EGON WERLICH

THE LEARNER'S VOCABULARY FOR TEXT ANALYSIS

VERLAG LAMBERT LENSING · DORTMUND

ISBN 3-559-23 201-5

11. Auflage 1979

Herstellung Ernst Knoth, Melle · Printed in Germany

ZIELSETZUNG UND GEBRAUCH DES WÖRTERBUCHES

Das hier vorgelegte *The Learner's Vocabulary for Text Analysis* ist eine Umarbeitung eines neuartigen Wörterbuchtyps: des vollständigen *Field System Dictionary for Text Analysis.* Es kann vorwiegend von der Mittelstufe an im Literaturunterricht benutzt werden. Obwohl um die Hälfte kürzer als die vollständige Ausgabe, hat das kleine Feldwörterbuch deren Gesamtanlage unverändert übernommen und ist in der Abfolge der Wort- und Kollokationsfelder * durchgehend sinnvoll geblieben. Auch die Zielsetzung dieses *The Learner's Vocabulary for Text Analysis* ist daher in den Grundzügen die gleiche: Es bietet dem Lernenden die Wörter des bedeutenden Wortschatzes der Textinterpretation in solchen Zusammenhängen an, die leichtes Behalten und Wiederholen, sachlich treffenden Wortgebrauch und reaktionssicheres, fließendes Sprechen in der Fremdsprache ermöglichen. Um das zu erreichen, ordnet dieses Wörterbuch alle Wörter systematisch in Sachzusammenhänge und sprachliche Feldzusammenhänge ein.

Im Überblick betrachtet, enthält die Anordnung der 12 Kapitel einen äußeren Rahmen (vgl. Kap. I–III und IX–XII), der das Vokabular zum jeweiligen Kunstwerk innerhalb einer der literarischen Gattungen (vgl. Kap. IV und V–VIII) umschließt. Die einleitenden Schritte des Leserzugangs zum Kunstwerk sind gewöhnlich durch einen allgemeineren Blickwinkel bestimmt. Die drei eröffnenden Kapitel geben darum jenes Vokabular, das der Leser für seine allgemeine Orientierung über Texte benötigt (I.), für das Eindringen in allgemeine Aspekte ihrer Darbietung (II.) und für die Erfassung ihrer strukturellen Organisation (III.). Da im Mittelpunkt eines jeden Kunstwerks der Mensch steht, gewinnt das umfangreiche Kapitel über *Characterization of Persons* (I, 2) grundlegende Bedeutung für jeden Interpretationsweg. Gerade in der Personencharakteristik kann die genaue Sachfeldaufgliederung zu einer sehr viel differenzierteren Sprachbeherrschung – und damit Wirklichkeitserfassung – führen (dem letztlich entscheidenden Ziel aller Literaturbetrachtung), als das mit den üblichen Wortzusammenstellungen bisher möglich war.

Den drei einleitenden Kapiteln folgt, was man als das Herzstück des Wörterbuches bezeichnen kann: die Kapitel zu den vier gesonderten literarischen Gattungen, denen die einzelnen Literaturwerke oder Texte, denen der Leser begegnet, zugeordnet werden können

---

* Zur Erläuterung dieser beiden zentralen Begriffe vgl. die Erklärung der Zeichen und Begriffe, S. 11.

(vgl. IV, 1; 2; 3; 4). Noch eng verknüpft mit diesen sind die Kapitel über Einzelaspekte, durch die die jeweiligen Texte einer Gattung charakterisiert sein können (V, VI, VII, VIII). Die vier abschließenden Kapitel des Rahmens führen wieder aus dem Literaturwerk und seinen Einzelaspekten hinaus: in den Wortschatz zu seinem Hintergrund (IX.; X.), seiner Veröffentlichung (XI.) und seinem Publikum (XII.).

Wie kann *The Learner's Vocabulary for Text Analysis* gebraucht werden? Seine systematische Anlage ermöglicht drei verschiedene Wege der Wortschatzerarbeitung, die getrennt oder miteinander verbunden verfolgt werden können:

1. die chronologische, Kapitel um Kapitel voranschreitende Erarbeitung, die den angebotenen Ordnungen der 12 Hauptkapitel und den darin enthaltenen Sinnzusammenhängen folgt *(the chronological approach);*
2. die kapitelweise Erarbeitung von einem Schlüsselbegriff oder einer Schlüsselvorstellung her, z. B. vom Stichwort *short story* her in Verbindung mit der Lektüre einer *short story* im Unterricht *(the conceptual approach);*
3. die gezielte Benutzung als literarisches Nachschlagewerk oder Sachwörterbuch, die anknüpft an ein einzelnes Schlüsselwort des literarischen Gegenstandsbereiches (z. B. an *style, metaphor* oder *climax*) und – nach Konsultierung des alphabetischen Index – hin zu Definitionen und bevorzugten sprachlichen Verbindungen (Kollokationen) im Wörterbuch führt *(the index approach).*

Innerhalb der einzelnen Felder kann der Lernende die genauere Erarbeitung noch einmal abstufen, indem er sich zunächst auf jene Wörter konzentriert, die als elementar *(elementary)* gekennzeichnet sind (halbfett gedruckt), und erst dann, in einem zweiten Arbeitsgang, auch alle als fortgeschritten *(advanced)* markierten Wörter (Normaldruck) miterfaßt. Eine wichtige allgemeine Orientierungshilfe geben dazu die beiden Teile des Inhaltsverzeichnisses. Der erste Teil *(A Survey)* vermittelt in einem Überblick dem Lernenden eine geordnete Vorstellung von den 12 wichtigsten sachlichen Einzelaspekten des Interpretationswortschatzes. Der zweite Teil *(A Systematic Index of Key Terms)* gibt eine klare Vorstellung von der feldmäßigen Aufgliederung jedes einzelnen Kapitels. So kann der Lernende schon nach kurzer Zeit über ein geistiges Ordnungsschema verfügen, mit dessen Hilfe er neue Wörter schnell in ihre sinngebende sprachliche Nachbarschaft stellen, sie so besser verstehen, daher auch besser behalten und schließlich treffender gebrauchen kann.

TABLE OF CONTENTS

A Survey

THE FIELD SYSTEM DICTIONARY

A Systematic Index of Key Terms

I. INTERPRETATION

1. Description

Some elements of description: Detail – nuances – tone – atmosphere – local colour
Account – record – diary – journal – minutes – report. Delineation – characterization

2. Characterization of persons

2.1 The outward appearance of persons

Physique: Characteristic features of a person's physique: Vigour / feebleness – fatness / thinness – tallness / shortness – health / sickness – dexterity / clumsiness
Physiognomy: A person's face: Shape – skin – complexion – facial expression / countenance – features / looks
The head: The skull – hair – forehead – eye-brows – eyes – nose – cheeks – mouth
Gestures and movements: Of the head / face / eyes . . . Of shoulders and arms. Of the hands / fingers. Of legs and feet
Gait: Manners of moving generally. Stride – step – pace. Verbs describing manners of walking: To walk / step / stride . . .
Posture: Position – carriage – attitude – bearing
Voice: Predominantly non-verbal kinds of utterances. Tones of voice

2.2 Drives and needs

Instinct – drive – need. Urge – motive – impulse. Motivation

2.3 Sense perception

Kinds of senses. Basic processes of sense perception: Sight – hearing – smell – touch – taste. Sub-sensory perception. The word family

2.4 Feeling

Feeling – emotion – mood

2.5 Understanding and thinking

Mind: States / frames of mind: Attentive – inattentive. Characteristics of an individual's mind
Understanding – consciousness
Intellect: Operations involving one's intellect – reason: Intellectual operations involving reason
Reasoning: Reasoning – thinking – thought (in the sense of thinking) – thought(s) (in the sense of idea) – idea
Intuition – knowledge: Basic processes connected with knowledge
The unconscious

2.6 Imagination

Imagination: Basic processes involving imagination – fancy – association
Memory – inspiration

2.7 Conscience

2.8 Dispositional aspects of personality

Personality – individual – person
Disposition – temper
Capacity: Intelligence – will (power). Capacity – ability (abilities) – aptitude
Trait: Dominant traits in persons
Habit
View: Attitude – view – opinion. Outlook – concept
Behaviour: Behaviour – manner – manners – tact
Character
Typology: Types according to the classical typology of temperaments. Types according to everyday language: Differences in outlook – in intelligence and knowledge – in generosity – in group dominance – in task solving

2.9 Visible action

Action – act – deed. Activity – performance – accomplishment – achievement

2.10 The individual in groups

Basic interpersonal behaviour patterns:
Acceptance – respect – admiration – trust – honesty – agreement – help – friendship – praise

Rejection – disrespect – contempt – mistrust – insincerity – disagreement – desertion – quarrel – reproof
Superiority – inferiority

3. Analysis

Criticism: The accomplishment of criticism. Kinds of criticism
Analysis – interpretation. Examination – study. Comment – evaluation. Explanation – paraphrase – summary

II. THE SPEAKER

Roles of the speaker. Point of view. Tone

III. COMPOSITION AND STRUCTURE

1. The organization of thought

Organization – structure – form – composition – compositional elements of a text

Arrangement – order – outline. Pattern

2. Stages in the succession of thoughts

The whole – subject / theme.

The thesis – exposition – argument – reason – condition. The proof – an example – a quotation – a citation

The antithesis – an objection – a contrast. A comparison – distinction – definition.

The synthesis – consequence – a transition
Conclusion – solution

IV. LITERARY GENRES

1. Fiction

Fiction
Novel: Types. Composition and component parts. Character. Plot. Setting. Language
Detective story. Science fiction. Popular / commercial fiction. Short story. Anecdote

2. *Drama*

Drama: Types. Theory of drama: The unities and catharsis
Tragedy – Comedy: Types
Drama, ctd.: The theme. Composition and component parts: General composition – dialogue – stage directions – exposition
Action. Plot. Character. The performance of plays – effect. The theatre building – stage – scenery – lighting – sound effects.
The actor – the audience

3. *Poetry*

The poem: Composition and component parts: The title – theme. The whole – division – stanzaic patterns – lines. Levels of meaning. Tone and style
Types of poems: The ballad – ode – elegy – sonnet
Some kinds of poetry: Light verse – the limerick – the clerihew

4. *Non-fiction*

Book-size types of non-fiction: The history – biography – autobiography
Shorter types of non-fiction: The treatise – dissertation – thesis – essay – paper – article

V. CONTENT AND MEANING

Content – contents – substance. Meaning – sense. Moral – lesson

VI. PROSODY

Prosody
Stanza: Basic stanza forms – verse – blank verse – free verse. Line – kinds of lines
Rhyme: Kinds of rhyme. Alliteration – assonance – consonance – onomatopoeia
Time: Time – rhythm: kinds of rhythm – cadence – metre: kinds of metre
Foot (measure). Stress: kinds of stress marks. Syllable

VII. LANGUAGE

Word: In a situation, from the speaker's point of view. From the listener's point of view
In the context of language generally: Word formation. The word as a sign. The linguistic history of words. Speech levels of words. The linguistic context of words. Words in a sentence. Punctuation in a sentence
Term: Term – expression – collocation – idiom – phrase – figure (of speech)
Vocabulary. Sentence. Language: Verbs describing the use of language: to utter / speak ... words
Speech. Meaning

VIII. STYLE

Style: Qualities of style usually considered good: Plainness. Conciseness. Clearness. Vigour. Elegance
Qualities of style usually considered bad: Ornament. Diffuseness. Obscurity. Feebleness. Inelegance
Diction
Basic stylistic devices: Figure of speech – image – pun. Comparison – metaphor – symbol. Personification – allegory. Repetition. Exaggeration – understatement – climax. Euphemism – paraphrase. Allusion – analogy – antithesis. Irony – parody – satire

IX. LITERARY HISTORY

Phases of literary history. Some literary epochs. Groupings of literary works

X. THE AUTHOR

Kinds of author. Authorship – talent – rank

XI. PUBLICATION

Publication. Parts of a book: The cover – jacket – printed pages
Kinds of book: Fact books – reference books – fiction books

XII. THE READER / LISTENER

Kinds of reader. Response. The effect of a work of verbal art on the reader

ERKLÄRUNG DER ZEICHEN UND BEGRIFFE

A. Zeichen

Der Schrägstrich (/) trennt Wörter, die in die Ordnung eines Wortfeldes gestellt sind. Jedes Wort der Reihe kann mit dem einführenden Verb und / oder der abschließenden Ergänzung gebraucht werden.

Der Gedankenstrich (–) trennt (1) Sinngruppen in großen Wortfeldern, (2) verschiedene *patterns* in einem Wortfeld.

Der doppelte Gedankenstrich (– –) trennt größere Wortgruppen innerhalb eines Wortfeldes von Schlüsselbegriffen, oder er markiert das Ende mehrerer Wortfelder, die unter einer eigenen Überschrift in Kollokationsfelder eingeschoben sind.

Drei Punkte (. . .) weisen auf Möglichkeiten, ein *pattern* oder eine Reihe auszudehnen oder fortzusetzen.

Ein Sternchen (*) zwischen Zeilen trennt Sinngruppen von Schlüsselbegriffen (die durch Gedankenstriche in einführenden Wortfeldern getrennt sind).

Großbuchstaben (VIGOROUS – FEEBLE) werden für Schlüsselwörter in verwandten Reihen von Wortfeldern gebraucht.

Kleine Großbuchstaben (DETAILS) werden für Schlüsselwörter und Überschriften gebraucht, die als untergliedernde Zwischenüberschriften in Kollokationsfeldern erscheinen.

Großer Halbfettdruck (**description**) wird für die bedeutendsten Schlüsselwörter im elementaren Vokabular eines Sachfeldes gebraucht.

Normaler Halbfettdruck wird gebraucht für Wörter, die als elementar in Sachfeldern (**account**) und Kollokationsfeldern (**to give . . . an account of**) gelten.

Normaltype wird gebraucht für Wörter, die als fortgeschritten in Kollokationsfeldern gelten (to present / render . . . an account of).

Großer Kursivdruck (*physiognomy*) wird gebraucht für die bedeutendsten Schlüsselwörter im fortgeschrittenen Vokabular eines Sachfeldes.

Kleiner Kursivdruck wird gebraucht (1) für Überschriften zu Unterabschnitten in Kollokationsfeldern (*some elements of description*), (2) für einzelne Schlüsselwörter des fortgeschrittenen Vokabulars (*record*) und (3) für das fortgeschrittene Vokabular in morphologischen Feldern (*to recount s. th.*).

B. Begriffe

Der Begriff

Wortfeld wird gebraucht für bedeutungsverwandte Wörter (**slender / slim / thin / lean,** etc.), die eine bestimmte Erscheinung (thinness) aus verschiedenen Blickwinkeln darstellen. Die leichten Bedeutungsunterschiede zwischen den einzelnen Wörtern eines Wortfeldes sind begründet sowohl durch die Sicht des Sprechers von der Erscheinung (**slim** [beschönigend] oder **thin** [abwertend]) wie durch die verschiedenen Aspekte, die die Erscheinung selbst darbietet.

Wortfamilie wird gebraucht für Wörter, die vom Stamm eines Schlüsselbegriffs abgeleitet und eng verwandt mit ihm sind. Sie bilden **morphologische Felder (to think, thinkable, unthinkable**).

Kollokationsfeld wird gebraucht für die bevorzugte sprachliche Umgebung (Kontext) eines Wortes. Das Kollokationsfeld wird gebildet von den verschiedenen Wortfeldern von Verben, Adjektiven, Substantiven und Präpositionen, die konventionell mit einem Allgemeinbegriff (**to walk / step / stride ...** mit **gait**) oder einem einzelnen Wort (**practical / theoretical / special ... knowledge**) zusammengehen.

I. INTERPRETATION

(1) Description

word field: **description** / **account** / record / diary / journal / minutes / **report** / epitome / **summary** / abstract / résumé / synopsis / digest / argument (Hauptinhalt eines Buches) / précis / excerpt / extract / **delineation** / sketch / **depiction** / portrayal / **characterization** / portrait / profile – **to describe** / record / **report** / **delineate** / sketch / **depict** / portray / **characterize s. th.** –
to caricature / distort s. th.

description

defining phrases: the term denotes s. th. pictured in words with varying degrees of accuracy (Beschreibung, Darstellung)

word family: to describe s. th. / description / descriptive / describable / indescribable

use (field of collocation):
to give a description of s. th.
to give **a(n) accurate** / faithful / lifelike / **factual** / **detailed** / circumstantial (ausführlich) / **vivid** (lebendig) / elaborate (sorgfältig ausgeführt) / mawkish (rührselig) ... **description**

some elements of description (also cf. III. composition and structure)
a description presents / contains many DETAILS / *nuances* ([njuːˈɑːnsiz] – Feinheiten) **of observation**
a description is written / given in a TONE **of** ... irony / contempt ...
it creates an ATMOSPHERE **of** ... / portrays *local colour* (i. e. it places emphasis on picturesque elements of a regional setting [Schauplatz, Hintergrund] such as landscape, dialect, or custom – Lokalkolorit)
to describe a person as ... (reliable ...) / **people of** ... **(courage** ...) / **scenes of** ... **(activity / misery** ...)
to read **a descriptive passage** in a book
to like descriptive writing

*

account
in the present context, denotes a more or less personal description of events (Bericht, Darstellung)
to give / present / render (wiedergeben) **an account of** (what happened ...)

to give a(n) eye-witness (Augenzeugen-) / first-hand / full-scale (vollständig) / engrossing (spannend) ... account
to *recount* s. th.

record ['rekɔːd]
is a written account of facts or events (schriftlicher Bericht; Protokoll)
to set down / keep / write a record of ...
to *record* [ri'kɔːd] an event (aufzeichnen)

a diary is a daily record of events and experiences (Tagebuch)
to keep / write a diary

a journal is a daily record of events less personal than the diary
minutes ['minits] (pl.) – ([Sitzungs]Protokoll)
to take / keep the minutes (P. führen)

report
is a general term for a formal account of events (Bericht, Referat)
to give / present / **write a report on a subject** / a war report
to report s. th.
it is reported that ...

*

delineation

denotes a description of s. th. in outline (skizzierende Beschreibung)
to give a delineation of s. th.
to delineate the features / characteristics of ...

characterization (also cf. I. 2. interpretation: characterization of persons)

denotes the description of the main or prominent features (hervorstechende Züge) of some person or object (Kennzeichnung, Charakterisierung)
to give a characterization of a person / an object
to characterize s. o. as ... (trustworthy ...)
to point out **the characteristics of**
to behave in a **characteristic** way
certain behaviour is characteristic of a person

(2) Characterization of Persons

(i) *The outward appearance of persons*

word field: physique ([fi'ziːk] – Körperbau, -beschaffenheit) / **constitution** (Körperbau in seiner anlagebedingten Gesundheit) / **physical**

condition (körperliche Verfassung, insbesondere des Augenblicks) / **body** / build / stature (['stætʃə] – Wuchs) / **figure** (Gestalt, Figur) / frame (Gestalt) / skeleton (Skelett, Knochengerüst)

physique

he is (sturdily . . .) built / put together
he is of / has a (sturdy . . .) constitution / make-up / build / frame
he is of / has (medium . . .) build / stature / height
he is of (strong . . .) physique
he is in / has a (good / bad . . .) physical condition

some characteristic features of a person's physique

vigour / feebleness – fatness / thinness – tallness / shortness – health / sickness – dexterity / clumsiness
to see a strong / VIGOROUS / stout (stämmig) **man**
to see a(n) athletic / muscular / sinewy (sehnig) / **wiry** (drahtig) man
a man has vigour / strength / energy / stamina (Widerstandskraft) / bounce (Schwung, Lebenskraft) / drive (Energie, Unternehmungsgeist) / verve (Feuer)
to be / see a man of infirm / **delicate** (zart) / FEEBLE (kraftlos) / frail (gebrechlich) physique
s. o. is a weak . . . man

to be / see a plump (rundlich, mollig) / massive / **paunchy** (dickbäuchig) / corpulent / FAT **man**
a man is getting gross / fat . . .
to be / see a slender (schlank, schmächtig) / slim (dünn) / THIN / lean (ds.) / gaunt (hager) / **skinny** (abgemagert) / scraggy (dürr) / bony / emaciated ([i'meiʃieitid] – abgezehrt) **man**

to be / see a TALL / erect / lanky (hoch aufgeschossen, schlaksig) / **big** / towering (hoch überragend) **man**
to see a SHORT / **small** / stumpy (gedrungen, untersetzt) / little / undersized (winzig) / dwarfish (zwergenhaft) **man**

to be / see a HEALTHY / **strong man**
to see a sickly / indisposed / SICK / senescent (alternd) / senile / **decrepit** (altersschwach, klapprig) **man**

to see a DEXTEROUS (geschickt, gelenkig) / **skilful man**
to see a CLUMSY (schwerfällig) / gawky (linkisch) **man**

physiognomy [fizi'ɔnəmi]

word field: physiognomy / **face** / **countenance** (Gesichtsausdruck) / **complexion** (Gesichtsfarbe, Aussehen) / **looks** (Aussehen) / features (Gesichtszüge) / lines (Falten) / **facial expression** / profile / grimace ([gri'meis] – Fratze)

defining phrases: physiognomy denotes the cast (Schnitt) / features (Züge) / looks of a person's face generally. It refers to a person's type of face (Gesichtsausdruck)
to describe a person's features / complexion / countenance / profile / looks

a person has a FULL / **chubby** (pausbäckig) / fleshy / plump / bloated (aufgedunsen) **face**
he has a(n) round / oval / long / large / small face
he has a(n) LEAN (mager) / hollow-cheeked / **wrinkled** (faltig, zerknittert) / **lined** (gefurcht) / rugged (['rʌgid] – durchfurcht) / withered (welk) **face**

a person looks . . . (pale . . .)
he has a (pale . . .) **complexion**
he has a SUNBURNT / **tanned** / bronzed **face**
he has a FAIR / **freckled** (sommersprossig) – DARK / **black face**
a person changes coulour
he turns red . . . / **grows pale** . . . / **loses colour**

the facial expression / countenance
to describe s. o.'s countenance / facial expression
a person has a blank face (ausdruckslos) / an air of . . . (superiority / importance . . . – überlegene / gewichtige Miene)
his face bears a (noble / detached . . .) **expression**
an expression of . . . (hate . . .) flickers across (huschen, zucken) / is on s. o.'s face
a person looks merry / **weary** (müde, matt) / **peevish** (mürrisch) / **sad** / dissipated (aufgelöst) / stern / grim . . . (also cf. I. 2. iv. feeling)
he makes a merry / **gay** / **wry** (schief) . . . **face**
he has / presents / displays (zur Schau tragen) **a sorrowful** / **sad . . . countenance**
his face is distorted (verzerrt) / contorted (ds.) in . . . (pain / anger . . .)

the features / looks of a face
a person is good-looking / better-looking than . . . / comely (of a woman's face and figure: anmutig) / **glamorous** (bezaubernd schön)
he has even (ebenmäßig) / **fine** / **handsome** (of men: hübsch) / **pretty** (of women: hübsch) / **beautiful** / strongly-marked / **proud** / **noble** / aristocratic – **ugly** (häßlich) / hideous **features**

the head

a person has a small / **big** / **large** / **massive** / well proportioned **head**
a person has fair / blonde / ginger (rötlichgelb) / **red** / **brown** / **dark** / **black** / **greying** / **grey** / **white** HAIR
his hair is dyed (gefärbt) black / blonde . . .

he has a high / low / broad / receding (fliehend) **/ wrinkled / furrowed** (durchfurcht) FOREHEAD (['fɔrid] – Stirn) or *brow* [au]
he has dark / bushy . . . (*eye*-)BROWS
a person has bright / gleaming **/ dreamy / hollow / small / big / large** EYES
he has a kind / keen (aufmerksam) / piercing (durchdringend) . . . **look** (Blick)
his eyes flash / blaze (flammen) with . . . (anger / fury)
he cries / weeps / wipes a tear from his eye
his eyes blink (at – blinzeln) / squint (at – schielen)
he is cross-eyed (schielt) / near-sighted / far-sighted / **blind**

a person has a small / big / short / long / flat (platt) NOSE
he has a straight (gerade) / **hooked** (Haken-) / **turned-up nose**
he is snub-nosed (stupsnasig) / hook-nosed / hawk-nosed / straight-nosed / flat-nosed (like a Negro)
a person has ruddy / rosy / blushed / flushed / feverish / **pale / hollow** (eingefallen) CHEEKS (Wangen)
his cheeks turn pale / red
he blushes (for shame . . .) – ([nach innen gewandt] rot werden) / **flushes** (crimson with irritation / disgust . . .) – ([nach außen gewandt] erröten)

a person has a thin-lipped / thick-lipped / tight (fest verschlossen) MOUTH
he has his mouth open / set tight
his mouth is distorted / contorted (in pain . . .)
the corners of his mouth are drawn upwards (in joy . . .) / downwards (in grief . . .)

gesture (and movements) – (Gebärde, Geste)

to make a gesture (in order to illustrate a point . . .)
to accompany / underline (unterstreichen) **one's words with a gesture of . . .**
to make a gesture of acceptance (Billigung) / refusal (Ablehnung) / rejection (ds.) to s. o.
a(n) fitting (passend) **/ expressive / vague** / ample (weitläufig) – **lively / graceful** (anmutig) **/ abrupt / impatient** / imperious (gebieterisch) **gesture**

gestures (and movements) of the head (face / eyes . . .)
to lift up / raise / drop (senken) **/ bend** (neigen) / incline / bow [bau] / **nod** (nicken) **/ shake** / turn aside **one's** HEAD
to make / pull a FACE
to frown (on . . . – die Stirn runzeln über) – to raise / knit (zus.-ziehen) / wrinkle one's *brows*

to look up / down / to the side
to look (over) **at s. o. / look away /** flinch (from ... – ausweichen) / glance backward at s. o.
to catch s. o. 's eye / **fix one's eyes on s. o.** (heften auf)
to give s. o. a furtive (verstohlen) / short / open / long glance or look
to look s. o. straight / squarely (direkt) in the face / eyes
to blink / wink (e. Auge zukneifen) at s. o.

gestures (and movements) of shoulders and arms
to raise / shrug (schütteln) / square (s. in d. Brust werfen) **one's** SHOULDERS
to turn one's back on s. o. / to s. o. (jd. den Rücken kehren)
to raise / lift / stretch out / reach out with / swing / **wave one's** ARM
to cross / fold one's arms
to embrace (umarmen) / hug s. o. (an s. drücken)

gestures (and movements) of the hands / fingers
to clap / stretch out / wave **one's** HANDS
to clasp (schließen) / fold (falten) / **join** / rub / wring one's hands
to slide (gleiten lassen) / dip (eintauchen) / plunge (versenken) one's hands into ... (a pocket ...)
to push s. th. away / aside
to snatch s. th. (from s. o.) – (wegschnappen) / **pull s. th.** / tug (zerren) at s. th. (s. o. 's hair) / **seize s. th.** (ergreifen) / clutch s. th. (packen, fest ergreifen)
to fight / struggle with
to shake hands with s. o. / grab s. o. by the arm or shoulder
to draw back one's hand
to stroke (streicheln) / run one's hand over s. th. / **pat** (tätscheln, klapsen) / caress ([kə'res] – liebkosen) s. o.
to slap (e. Klaps geben) / **hit / smack** (ohrfeigen) / **strike / beat** s. o.
to point one's FINGER / **fore-finger** / thumb **at s. o. / s. th.**
to wag one's finger at s. o. (mit d. Finger drohen) / put one's finger to one's lips
to touch (berühren) / handle (anfassen) / pinch (kneifen) / squeeze (drücken) / scratch (kratzen) s. th. / s. o.
to snap one's fingers (schnalzen mit)
to tap one's forehead (s. an d. Stirn tippen)
to clench (ballen) / **unclench one's fist**
to pound / knock / beat / thump (hämmern) **one's fists against**
to bang at ... (a door) with one's fist
to shake one's fist at s. o.

gestures (and movements) of legs and feet
to cross one's legs (übereinanderschlagen)

to kneel down before . . . / bend one's knee to . . . (s. o.)
to stamp one's feet (mit den Füßen stampfen) / trample on / tread on (treten auf) s. th.
to slip on s. th. (ausgleiten, -rutschen) – scramble to one's feet (s. aufrappeln) / get to one's feet / stand up

gait

denotes a person's specific or characteristic manner of walking (Gang, Gangart, Haltung)

manners of moving generally
a person has a manner of moving / walking
he has a walk / gait
he has / moves / walks with **a(n)** LIGHT / **easy** / brisk (flott) / elastic / elegant / mincing (geziert) **gait**
he has a(n) HEAVY / **stiff** / **proud** / noble / imposing (eindrucksvoll) **gait**
he moves with energetic STRIDES (langer Schritt) / a loose stride
he moves with small steps (kleiner, eiliger Schritt)
he moves at a (quick / brisk . . .) PACE (Schritt, Schrittempo)

some verbs describing manners of walking
to walk ([zu Fuß] gehen) / **step** / **stride (out)** / **pace (up and down** – auf- und abwandern) / stalk (steifbeinig gehen, stolzieren) / strut (einherstolzieren)
to go for / **have** / **take a walk** (spazieren gehen)
to **stumble** (stolpern) / **stagger** (taumeln)
to hasten / scamper (hasten) / **hurry** / **run** / **dash** (stürmen) / dart (off – davonstürzen) / **rush** (rasen, dahinjagen) / race (dahinrasen, -schießen) / fly

posture

word field: **posture** / **position** / **attitude** / pose / bearing / carriage / deportment

defining phrases: the term denotes the general or specific position / attitude of a person's whole body ([bestimmte] Haltung, Stellung)

use (field of collocation):
to take / adopt / assume **a posture** of
to have / hold / maintain **a posture** of
he has / holds **a(n) uncomfortable** / **awkward** / humble / **unnatural posture**

position
denotes a relatively stable situation of the human body or a stable arrangement of the limbs (Lage)
to be in a particular position

carriage
denotes the manner in which a person holds himself naturally while walking or standing (Körperhaltung, Gang)
to have a(n) upright / graceful . . . carriage
to *carry* oneself / one's head in a characteristic / noble . . . way
to carry oneself erect

attitude
denotes a bodily position that expresses some condition of a person's mind (Haltung)
to have / assume a(n) (friendly / aggressive . . .) attitude
bearing
denotes a noble attitude (of both body and mind) – (Auftreten, Verhalten)
a person has the bearing of . . . (a soldier / gentleman . . .)
he is a person of . . . (noble / dignified / soldierly . . .) bearing
to *bear* oneself like . . . (a soldier / gentleman . . .)

voice – (Stimme)

word field: **utterance** (Äußerung) / **sound** (Laut) / articulation / **noise** (Geräusch)
word family: voice / to voice s. th. (a complaint) – (zum Ausdruck bringen) / voiceless / voiced (consonants)
use (field of collocation):
breathing and voice
a person **breathes** (atmen) – **breathes in** (ein-)
he produces sounds from his throat and mouth
he utters sounds / has a voice
he raises (lauter sprechen) / lowers / drops his voice
predominantly non-verbal kinds of utterances
(for verbs describing the use of language cf. VII. language)
a person shouts at the top of his voice / bawls (grölen) / rants (toben, brüllen)
he grunts ([ärgerlich] grunzen) / gives a(n) (amused . . .) grunt / burps (aufstoßen) / belches (rülpsen) / gargles (gurgeln) / hiccups (['hikʌps] – den Schluckauf haben) / gulps (würgen) / **coughs** ([kɔfs] – husten) / sneezes (niesen) / yawns (gähnen) / purrs (vor Behagen summen) / hums (summen) / whistles (pfeifen, flöten)
he speaks in a low voice – hisses (zischen) / **whispers**
he mumbles (undeutlich murmeln) / **murmurs** (sanft u. leise murmeln) / coos (of babies: ds.) / mutters (leise murmeln) / grumbles (ärgerlich brummen)
he lisps (lispeln) / stutters (stottern) / stammers (ds.)

he sighs (seufzen) / **moans** (stöhnen, jammern) / **groans** (ächzen) / **sobs** (schluchzen) / **cries** / **weeps** / blubbers (heulen) / whines (winseln) / whimpers (wimmern)
he has a(n) soft / **harsh** (schroff) / **sharp** / **loud** / **dark** / **coarse** (rauh) / **high-pitched** (hoch) / **feeble . . . voice**

(ii) *Drives and needs*

word field: reflex / **instinct** / **drive** / **need** / **desire** (Begierde) / appetite (Verlangen, Gelüst) / tendency / urge / compulsion / craving / striving / **motive** / incentive / impulse / **motivation**

instinct – (Instinkt)

to arouse the maternal (Mutter-) / **paternal** / **collecting instinct**
to produce an instinctive reaction / **response** from
to act by instinct / **instinctively**

drive – (Antrieb, Trieb)

to stimulate / activate / relieve (erleichtern) / gratify (befriedigen) / **satisfy** (ds.) **a drive**
primary drives are **the hunger drive** / **parental drive** / **drive for self-preservation** (Selbsterhaltungstrieb) / **sex drive**
to have inborn (angeboren) / **innate** (ds.) / native (ds.) / congenital (ds.) **drives**
man is driven by . . . (instincts . . .) / **towards a certain behaviour** / to behave in a certain way

need

denotes a condition in which the individual feels want of (Mangel an) something – (Bedürfnis)
to feel / meet / **answer** / serve / relieve / **satisfy** / **fulfil a need**
man has a bodily /physiological **need for air** / **food** / **exercise** / **rest** / **sleep**
excretion / urination are bodily needs

urge

denotes a strong drive or tendency towards some behaviour or performance (Ausführung einer Handlung) – (Drang)
to feel / be driven by an urge to do s. th. / towards some action
to be / **feel urged to do s. th.**

*

motive – (Bewegung, Motiv)

to have a motive for some action / for **doing s. th.**
to be driven to some action / actuated by a motive of . . .
to do s. th. /**act from motives of . . .** (hatred / love . . .)

impulse
denotes a sudden stimulus to action without deliberation (Überlegung) – (plötzliche Regung, Impuls)
to act on impulse / on the impulse of the moment / on the spur of the moment

motivation – (Begründung, Motivierung, Motivation)

to have a specific motivation for doing s. th.
a person's motivation for some action is . . . (envy . . .)
to be motivated / actuated **to an action by** a drive for . . . (recognition / acceptance / security . . .)

(iii) *Sense perception*

sense perception – (Sinneswahrnehmung)

kinds of senses
man receives / is given information about the world through his senses / sense-organs (Sinnesorgane)
he receives information through **external senses** (which respond to stimuli from outside) – through **the basic senses of sight / hearing / smell / touch / taste**
he has a(n) optic (visual) / auditory (relating to hearing) / **olfactory** (relating to smell) / **tactual** (relating to touch) / **gustatory** (relating to taste) sensation or **sense impression**
man has a number of sub-senses
he has body senses such as **the sense of hunger / thirst / movement**
he has an aesthetic sense – a sense of art / music . . . – taste

some basic processes of sense perception
sight
to sight / catch sight of / catch a glimpse of (e. flüchtigen Blick erhaschen von) / **notice** / observe (bemerken) / behold (liter.) / make out / **perceive** (wahrnehmen) s. th.
to eye / **view** / scan (forschend überblicken) / survey **s. th.**
to glance at / peep at (verstohlen anblicken) / pry into (neugierig gucken, schnüffeln) **s. th.**
to see / look at / watch / observe (beobachten) / **peer at** (genau begucken) / **gaze at** (bestaunen, anstarren) / **gape at** (angaffen) **s. th.**
to inspect / examine / scrutinize (genau prüfend ansehen) **s. th.**
to blink (anblinzeln) / **wink** (e. Auge zukneifen) / **squint at s. o.** (anschielen)
s. th. is visible / invisible

hearing
to hear / attend to / **give attention to / overhear** (belauschen, zufällig mit anhören) **s. th.**

to listen to (zuhören) **s. th.**
s. th. is audible / inaudible

smell
to smell (an aroma / a scent [Duft] . . .) / scent (as of dogs: wittern) **s. th.**
s. th. is fragrant (wohlriechend) with / **sweet-smelling – bad-smelling / stinking** . . .

touch
to touch / finger (befingern) / **handle** (anfassen, hantieren mit) **s. th.**
to feel s. th. (befühlen)
s. th. is sharp / blunt (stumpf) – **smooth** (glatt) / glossy (glatt, blank) / **coarse** (grob, rauh) – **even** (eben) / **uneven** (to the feel)

taste
s. th. tastes of (schmeckt nach) / has a flavour of (Aroma)
s. th. is acid (sauer) / **sour** / **sharp** / hot (sehr scharf) / piquant (['piːkənt] – pikant) / **sweet** / insipid (ohne Geschmack, fade)

sub-sensory perception
to feel warm – to **sweat** ([e] – schwitzen) / perspire (ds.) – **feel cold** – to **shiver** (frösteln) / **shudder** (erzittern, schaudern) / **tremble** (beben) / quiver / shake (**at s. th. / with cold** . . .)
to feel hungry / thirsty / satiated (['seiʃieitid] with – gesättigt)
to feel giddy (schwindelig) / dizzy (benommen) / dazed (ds.)
to feel worn (abgespannt) / **tired** / fatigued / worn out (zermürbt) / **exhausted / faint** (matt, der Ohnmacht nahe)

the word family
sensory is used with reference to what affects (berühren, ansprechen) the sense-organs (n. *sensation* – Sinneswahrnehmung, -empfindung)
sensory perception / experience

sensitive refers to the capacity of responding to particular degrees of various kinds of stimuli (empfindsam, empfindlich) – (n. *sensitivity* or *sensitiveness* – Empfindlichkeit)
man's eyes are sensitive to light
he is sensitive to praise / criticism / blame (Tadel)

sensual refers to an excessive appetite (übertriebene Gier) for pleasant sensations (connected with drink / food / sex / drugs) – (n. **sensuality** – Sinnlichkeit)
to pursue sensual pleasures

(iv) *Feeling*

word field: **feeling / emotion / disturbance** (Beunruhigung) / perturbation (Bestürzung, Unruhe) / **confusion** (Verwirrung) / commotion (Erschütterung) / **agitation** (heftige Bewegung) / **alarm** (Bestürzung, Angst) – affect (Gemütsbewegung) / affection(s) (Gemütsbewegung; Zuneigung, Liebe) – **mood** (Stimmung) – **sentiment** (Gefühlsregung)

feeling

refers to psychic processes which man is subjected to or seized by (Gefühl, Empfindung)
to have / show / be seized by / experience / be attacked by / be subjected to / suffer / be overcome by / be overpowered by / be overwhelmed by (überwältigen) / **be inflamed with a feeling of ...** (anger / disgust ...)
to have a passing / fleeting (flüchtig) / **subtle** (fein) **feeling that ...** (s. th. is about to / is to / will happen)
to show little / much / excessive (übertrieben) / **no feeling towards ...**
to control / restrain (bezähmen) / constrain (zwingen) / **suppress one's feelings**
to stir / arouse (wecken) / **excite** (erregen) / **evoke** / generate **feelings of ... / over s. th.**
to feel with / for s. o.

*

emotion

denotes a strong feeling (Rührung, Gemütsbewegung, [Gefühls-] Regung)
to be seized / overcome by an emotion of
to be kindled by (anreizen, entflammen) / **filled with** / imbued with (durchdrungen von) **an emotion of ... (love / joy / fear ...)**

mood

denotes a balanced state (ausgeglichener Zustand) of particular feelings which lasts for some time – (Stimmung, Laune)
to be in a particular mood
to be in a(n) peaceful / irritable (gereizt) / **merry / cheerful / joking** / sombre (düster) **mood**
to be in the mood to do s. th. / for s. th. (Lust haben zu)
to be in no mood for s. th. (keine Lust haben)

(v) *Understanding and thinking*

word field: psyche (['saiki] – Seele) / **soul** (Seele, Gemüt) / **mind / understanding / consciousness / brain** (Verstand, Kopf) / **intellect** / mentality (Denkungsart, Gesinnung) / cognition / **reason / thought (thinking) / thought(s) (idea) / intuition / knowledge** / the preconscious / **the unconscious** / the collective unconscious – –
psychic(al) / mental (of or in the mind) – (geistig, Geistes-) / spiritual (having intelligence and will, but no body) – (geistig, unkörperlich)

mind – (Geist, Seele)

to have / **show presence** (Geistesgegenwart) / keenness (Geistesschärfe) **of mind**
to reveal / gain knowledge of the states / processes / operations / workings of the mind
s. th. comes to one's mind
to keep one's mind on s. th.
to keep / **bear s. th. in mind**
to set one's mind on doing s. th. (s. etwas fest vornehmen)
to distract one's mind
to make up / follow / **change one's mind**
s. th. passes out of / slips from (entfallen) one's mind
s. o. is not in his right mind – **he is** tipsy (angeheitert) / **drunk** / **mad**
he has gone out of his mind / **gone mad**

to describe a person's mental states / **processes ...**
to have / suffer a *mental breakdown* (Geisteszs.bruch)
s. o. shows (exceptional ...) mental agility – is mentally retarded (geistig zurückgeblieben)

states / frames of mind
to be in a ... (cheerful ...) state / **frame of mind** (Geistesverfassung)
to be ATTENTIVE **(to** – aufmerksam) / observant (of – ds.) / awake to (s. e. Sache bewußt sein) / alive to (achtsam auf) / circumspect (umsichtig) / receptive (of – aufnahmefähig)
to be INATTENTIVE / unobservant / **absent-minded** (geistesabwesend) / **distracted** (abgelenkt) / abstracted (zerstreut) / **bored** (gelangweilt)

characteristics of an individual's mind
to be high- (hochherzig) / **open-** / strong- / serious- / **single-** (zielbewußt) / career- / **narrow-** (engstirnig) / **absent-** / low- / **evil-minded**
to attribute s. th. to **narrow-** / **absent- ... mindedness**

*

understanding – (Verstehen, Verstand)

word field: **understanding** / **comprehension** (Begriffsvermögen, Verständnis) / apprehension (ability to understand) – (Fassungskraft, Begreifen) / **grasp** (Verständnis) – incomprehension / misapprehension

word family: **to understand s. th.** / **be understandable** / **to misunderstand s. th.**

use (field of collocation):
to be quick / **slow of understanding** / **comprehension** / apprehension / **grasp**

to understand s. th. / make oneself understood
to understand s. th. by a term / word / phrase . . .

consciousness

denotes the waking mind's awareness (Bewußthaben) of all its processes and contents, if it pays attention to them (Bewußtsein)
to be without / have no consciousness . . . (during sleep . . .)
to have no consciousness of s. th. happening / do s. th. without consciousness
to lose / recover / regain consciousness
to be aware of one's stream of consciousness (Bewußtseinsstrom)
to be conscious of / aware of / awake to / **know about s. th.**
to be keenly / acutely / sharply – hardly / scarcely **conscious of s. th.** (certain sensations)
to be unconscious of s. th.

*

intellect

word field: **intellect** / mentality / acuteness (Scharfsinnigkeit) / acumen ([–'– –] – Scharfsinn) / esprit / wit / sagacity (Scharfsinn, Klugheit) / subtlety (ds.) / **discrimination** (Unterscheidungsvermögen) / discernment (Scharfblick, Urteilskraft) / **judgment** / judiciousness (Klugheit, Einsicht) / discretion (Besonnenheit, Klugheit) – –
stupidity / dullness – –
stupid / dull . . .

defining phrases: intellect refers to the operations that produce knowledge of facts or ideas (whereas *intelligence* refers to the innate capacity of knowing how to do and exploit s. th.) – (Denkvermögen, Intellekt, Verstand)

word family: **intellectual** adj. / an **intellectual** / intelligible

use (field of collocation):

to exercise one's intellect on a problem . . .
to have / **possess** / be possessed of **a(n) quick** / **sharp** / acute / **highly developed** – **weak intellect**

some operations involving one's intellect

to perceive / apprehend **s. th.**
to see (verstehen) / **realize** (klar erkennen) / **understand** / **comprehend** (begreifen) **s. th.**
to distinguish / discriminate (Unterschiede machen) **between things**
to compare two things – **one thing with another** (of the same class) / **to another** (of a different class)
to contrast one thing with another

to explain / **interpret** / construe (auslegen, deuten) / **analyze** / **elucidate** (erhellen) / evaluate (bewerten) **s. th.**
to confuse s. th. with (verwechseln)
man is an intellectual being
he possesses intellectual powers / faculties / capacities / flexibility

reason

word field: **reason** / **reasoning** (Denken, Schlußfolgern) / **thinking** / **thought** – –
rational (vernunftmäßig) / **irrational**

defining phrases: reason, in the present context, denotes either the higher intellectual operations generally (Vernunft), or the capacity for explicit thought towards a goal (Verstand)

word family: **reason** / **to reason** (logisch denken, folgern) / **reasoning** / **reasonable** / **unreasonable** (unvernünftig)

use (field of collocation):
man has / **is endowed with reason**
he applies his reason to . . . (a problem / an objective . . .)
he listens to / hears / submits to / yields to (Vernunft annehmen) **reason**

some basic intellectual operations involving reason
to think – think of / **about s. th.**
to think s. th. out (ausdenken) / **over** (über-)
to reflect on s. th. / meditate on s. th. / ponder over s. th. (nachsinnen, -grübeln) / brood over (brüten, grübeln) s. th.
to speculate (Vermutungen anstellen) / muse (in Gedanken versunken sein)
to advance reasonable / **unreasonable arguments** / demands / terms

*

reasoning

refers to a process of thinking with a conclusion (Denken, Schlußfolgern)
to show / exhibit power of reasoning
to pursue a(n) new / absurd / convincing . . . **line of reasoning**
inductive / deductive reasoning

thinking

word field: **thinking** / cogitation (Nachdenken, Denkfähigkeit) / reflection / contemplation (Nachsinnen, Nachdenken) / deliberation (Überlegen, Überlegung) / **consideration** (ds., Erwägung) / speculation / **musing** (Grübeln, Sinnen) / meditation *defining phrases: thinking* denotes a course of ideas generally, especially one produced by a problem (Denken)

word family: **to think of / about s. th. – thinkable / unthinkable**

use (field of collocation):

to do some (hard ...) **thinking (on a problem** / matter ...)

s. th. is the (dominant ...) **line / course / train / trend / way of thinking** / thought

to think in abstractions / generalizations ...

to think hard – consider / **reflect on** / **deliberate** (überlegen) / contemplate / brood over / cogitate upon / **figure s. th. out** (ausrechnen, rauskriegen) / work s. th. out / speculate on s. th.

thought (in the sense of thinking)

word field: **thinking** / cogitation (Nachdenken, Denkfähigkeit) / **reflection** / contemplation (Nachdenken, Nachsinnen) / deliberation (Überlegen, Überlegung) / **consideration** (ds., Erwägung) / speculation / **musing** (Grübeln, Sinnen) / meditation

defining phrases: used only in the singular, *thought* refers to the process or way of thinking generally (Denken, Gedanken[welt])

word family: **thought / thought**(s) / **thoughtful / thoughtless**

use (field of collocation):

to give / devote (widmen) (some / little ...) **thought to a matter**

to be deep / absorbed / **lost** / buried **in thought**

thought(s) (in the sense of idea)

word field: **idea** / notion (unbestimmte Vorstellung) / **concept** (Vorstellung, Begriff)

defining phrases: used both in the singular and the plural, the term refers to single ideas or to a chain of reasoning (Gedanke[n])

use (field of collocation):

a thought (sg.) suddenly **enters one's mind / strikes one**

a thought suggests itself / presents itself / **occurs to s. o.**

it rises to / **crosses** / flashes across / **passes through** (geht e. durch den Kopf) **one's mind**

it occupies (beschäftigt) / **oppresses** (bedrückt) **one's mind**

s. th. is / comes as a stray (beiläufig) / sobering (ernüchternd) thought

a person's one thought is how / when / where to do s. th.

to have *obsessive thoughts* (Zwangsvorstellungen) / add an *afterthought* to (nachträglicher Einfall) / have *second thoughts*

s. th. comes as an afterthought to / as a rider on (Zusatz) ...

to be thoughtful (of s. th.) / thoughtless (inconsiderate)

to blame / forgive s. o. for his *thoughtlessness*

idea – (Vorstellung, Eingebung)

word field: **idea** / **thought** / **concept** / conception / notion / preoccupation – (Voreingenommenheit) / **obsession** – (Zwangsvorstellung, Besessenheit)

use (field of collocation):

to get / acquire / form an idea of s. th.
to form a general / correct / wrong . . . idea of s. th.
to have an / no / not the slightest idea about s. th. / of s. th.
to favour (befürworten) / approve – disapprove / **reject an idea doing s. th. / that is a good / not a bad idea**
to pronounce (verkünden) / **express** / commit to paper / **spread** (verbreiten) / propagate **one's ideas**
to have a fixed idea (an emotionally deeply entrenched thought which recurs and persists) / **preconceived ideas** (vorgefaßte Vorstellungen)

intuition – (unmittelbare Erkenntnis, Eingebung, Intuition)

use (field of collocation):
to go / work by intuition
to have / posses / gain intuitive knowledge of s. th.

knowledge – (Wissen, Kenntnis)

word field: **knowledge** / **experience** (Erfahrung) / **memories** (Erinnerungen) / **insight into** – **learning** (Gelehrsamkeit) / erudition (ds., Belesenheit) / **experience** (Kenntnis) / acquaintance with / **familiarity with** / proficiency (Können) / **skill** / command of (Beherrschung) / expertise ([ˌekspəːˈtiːz] – Sachkenntnis) / **expert knowledge** / previous experience (Vorkenntnisse) – –
omniscience (Allwissenheit) – **ignorance** (Unwissenheit) / nescience (vollständige Unwissenheit)

word family: **to know s. th.** / be in the know (eingeweiht sein) / **knowledge** / foreknowledge (Vorherwissen) / **know-how**

use (field of collocation):
to have / posses / display / **lack knowledge of s. th.**
to get / obtain / gain / acquire (depth and breadth of) knowledge
to increase (erweitern) / **expand / brush up** (auffrischen) / polish up (ds.) **one's knowledge**

some basic processes connected with knowledge
to get to know / **know / see / realize / be aware of / be familiar with /** be acquainted with / **have been informed of s. th.**
to know s. th. for a fact (als Tatsache) / s. o. by name / s. o. by sight
to be (well) versed / unversed (unbewandert) in a field of knowledge

to be ignorant of / unaware of / unfamiliar with / unacquainted with
to be sure / assured of (überzeugt sein) / **certain of s. th.**
to doubt s. th. – be unassured of / uncertain of s. th.
to have practical / theoretical / special / intimate / extensive / **superficial knowledge**
s. th. is common knowledge (allgemein bekannt) / **belongs to general knowledge** (Allgemeinwissen)

*

the unconscious
refers to that part of one's mental structure and activity of which one is unaware. It influences conscious processes and can be detected (entdecken) and partially understood through the analysis of behaviour / associations / dreams and mental disorders (das Unbewußte)
to act from unconscious motivations / drives / urges / needs
to be / lie unconscious

(vi) *Imagination*

word field: **imagination / fancy / fantasy** / reverie / delusion / **illusion** / fiction / wishful thinking / make-believe / caprice / **whim** / ingenuity (Erfindungsgabe) / **creativity / originality** – –
association / memory / foresight / **inspiration** / prescience (Vorherwissen, Voraussicht) – –
imaginary / fictitious / fantastic / illusory / ideal

imagination

refers to the creative power of the mind to form or recall an image of external objects in the mind
Imagination is based on what is known (Einbildungs-, Vorstellungskraft; Phantasie)
to have / possess imagination
one's imagination is stirred / affected / **caught** / captured / **held**
some basic processes involving imagination
to have / see / picture / conjure up (['kʌndʒə] – heraufbeschwören) **s. th. before one's imagination / mind's eye**
to imagine / figure (s. ausmalen) / visualize (s. vergegenwärtigen) / envisage (doing s. th.) – (ins Auge fassen) **s. th.**
to imagine / fancy **that . . .** (one sees a dragon)
to be *imaginative* in picturing / doing s. th.
to imagine s. th. / oneself doing s. th.

fancy

denotes a form of relatively undirected, playful imagination
Fancy produces pleasing / graceful / odd mental images (Einbildung, Phantasie)
to take / tickle / **catch** / **hold a person's fancy**
to have strange . . . fancies about s. th.
a character in fiction is a figure of fancy
one *fancies* that one is . . . (sich vorstellen, einbilden)
illusion – (Illusion, Trugbild)
to have / create / entertain (hegen) / **have few** / **have no illusions about s. th.** / **of** . . . (escape . . .)
s. th. (success / victory . . .) **is illusory**

association – (Vorstellungsverknüpfung, Assoziation)

to link / connect impressions / ideas by association
to call forth / stir / arouse / evoke **associations** by a stimulus
s. th. **is regularly associated with** a particular response

*

memory – (Gedächtnis, Erinnerungsvermögen)

word field: **memory** / recollection (Gedächtnis[vermögen]) / remembrance (Gedächtnis, Gedanken) / **reminiscence** ([Lebens-]Erinnerung) / **learning** ([Er]-Lernen) / retention (Merkfähigkeit, Behaltenkönnen) / **recognition** ([Wieder]-Erkennen) – –
forgetting (Vergessen) / **forgetfulness** (Vergeßlichkeit) – –
to be forgetful / oblivious of **s. th.** (etw. vergessen haben)
word family: to memorize s. th. (s. einprägen, auswendig lernen) / **memory** / **memoirs** (Memoiren) / memorial (Denkmal)
use (field of collocation):
to have a good / photographic / **bad memory** (**for** names . . .)
to speak / **quote** (zitieren) **from (or by) memory**
to reconstruct s. th. from memory
to commit s. th. (a text) to memory / **learn s. th. by heart** / to learn s. th. by rote (rein mechanisch)
to retain (behalten, s. merken) an idea of s. th. / **to keep s. th. in mind** / to store information
to forget s. th.
to know / **remember** (s. erinnern an) / **recall** (s. in die Erinnerung rufen) / **be reminded of** (erinnert werden an) **s. th.**
an idea recurs (wiederkehren) to / comes back to (einfallen) one's mind
to recollect s. th. (s. ins Gedächtnis zurückrufen, s. besinnen auf)

to have a(n) good / active / trained / retentive / powerful / excellent **memory**
to have a poor / **bad** / short / feeble / unreliable **memory**
to have dim (blaß, schwach) memories of s. th.

inspiration – (Eingebung, Inspiration)

to work / write / speak under inspiration
to have a flash of inspiration
to be inspired to / by / with s. th.
s. th. (a feeling) is inspired in a person
to be drug- (opium- / LSD- . . .) inspired

(vii) *Conscience*

word field: **conscience** / super-ego (Über-Ich) / **inner voice** / **scruples** (Bedenken) / qualms ([ɑː] – Bedenken) – –
sense of duty / obligation / **responsibility** / **guilt** / regret / penitence (Reue, Bußfertigkeit) – –
remorse (at – Reue) / **repentance** (of – Bereuen) / contrition (Zerknirschung) / compunction (Gewissensbisse, Reue) – –
sin / **vice** (Laster) / **virtue** (Tugend)

conscience – (Gewissen)

to have s. th. on one's conscience
to feel pangs / pricks / stings / prickings / twinges **of conscience** (Gewissensbisse)
to feel guilty – **innocent** (unschuldig)
to feel regret / penitence / **remorse**
s. th. troubles / alarms / torments (quälen) / tortures (foltern) **one's conscience**
to be compelled to a confession by one's conscience

to suppress the voice of conscience
to calm / tranquillize (beruhigen) / soothe (beschwichtigen) / salve (ds.) / discharge (entlasten) / do violence (Gewalt antun) **to one's conscience**
to feel tempted (in Versuchung geraten)
to be sorry for / **repentant** (**of** – reuig) / penitent (reuig, zerknirscht) – **unrepentant** / impenitent

to have a sensitive (empfindlich) / scrupulous **conscience**
to have a(n) easy / elastic (weit) / indifferent / **insensitive** / obdurate (verstockt) **conscience**
to have a(n) good / clear / free / quiet / **calm conscience**
to have a(n) guilty / **troubled** / agitated / tormented / tortured **conscience**

(viii) *Dispositional aspects of personality*

Personality

word field: **personality** / **individual** / individuality / **person** / personage / **self** / ego

personality – (Person, Persönlichkeit)

someone is / **has a personality**
he has a(n) remarkable / **interesting** / striking / outstanding **personality**

individual – (Individuum, der Einzelne)

to protect / safeguard (sichern) the rights of the individual
individuals make up a family / group / crowd ...

person – (Person, Einzelwesen)

to meet a(n) young / **middle-aged** / **old person**
persons in the plural are referred to as **people** (Leute)
to become personal / have a personal grudge against s. o.

Disposition

word field: **disposition** / predisposition / **bent** / propensity / **inclination** / leaning (Neigung) / turn / **bias** / **temperament** / **temper**

disposition – (Neigung, natürliche Veranlagung)

to be of a particular (generous / mean ...**) disposition**
to be ... (generous / mean ...**) in disposition**
to be some type ... (a daredevil / coward ...**) by disposition**
to have / **show** / **possess a disposition to** do s. th.

inclination

denotes a dispositional mental *leaning* towards, or a momentary liking for, s. th. (Neigung, Vorliebe)
to have an / **no inclination to do s. th.**
to follow / act according to / indulge (fröhnen) **one's inclinations**
to be inclined / **prone to do s. th.**

*

temper

denotes either the same as temperament (Temperament, Leidenschaftlichkeit) or the degree of an individual emotional state of mind (Naturell; Gemütsart; Laune)
to be in a good / **bad temper**
to get / fly into a temper (in Wut geraten)
to lose / **keep one's** (ruhig bleiben) **temper**
to be in a / out of (wütend sein) temper

to be of even / mild / stolid (stur) / clement ([ˈklemənt] – nachsichtig) / genial – **uneven** / **fierce** / **aggressive . . . temper** (temperament)

to be good- / sweet- / short- / hot- / fiery- / **bad-** / **ill-tempered**

Capacity

word field: **intelligence** / **will** (power) / **capacity** / **ability** / flair / **aptitude** / faculty (Vermögen, Anlage)

intelligence

word field: **intelligence** / **understanding** / **insight** (Verständnis, Einblick) / discrimination (Scharfblick) / **common sense** (gesunder Menschenverstand) / brains (Köpfchen, Verstand) / **cleverness** (Klug-, Gescheitheit) / prudence (Vorsicht, Klugheit) / acumen ([əˈkjuːmən] – Scharfsinn) / penetration (ds., durchdringender Verstand) / **subtlety** (Scharfsinnigkeit) / **know-how** (praktisches Wissen)

defining phrases: the term denotes an individual's capacity for grasping (begreifen) relationships or his thinking and learning capacity generally (Intelligenz)

word family: **intelligent** (knowing how) / intelligentsia (die Gebildeten)

use (field of collocation):

to have / **possess** / **be endowed with** (begabt mit) / be gifted with (**average** / superior . . .) **intelligence**

to be deficient in (Mangel haben) / **lack intelligence**

to test / determine / measure **a person's intelligence**

to be dull / poor / retarded (zurückgeblieben) / below average / **average** / **bright** (gescheit, aufgeweckt) / **outstanding** / exceptional **intellectually**

to have a practical / common-sense / **theoretical** / **critical intelligence**

to be intelligent / **unintelligent**

the *intellectual* grasp of a rule (cf. intellect, p. 26) does not necessarily involve its *intelligent* application

will (power) – (Wille)

to have / **posses a strong** / **weak will**

to show will power / **strength of will** / resolution / perseverance / tenacity / **initiative** / **energy** / **purpose** / **weakness of will**

to make a weak / **strong effort of will** (Willensanstrengung)

to have free will / **freedom of will**

to do s. th. of one's own (free) will

some processes and states involving will power

to want / **wish** / **intend** / **plan** / **decide** (s. entschließen) / **make up one's mind** (beschließen) **to do s. th.**

to do s. th. intentionally / **on purpose** (mit Absicht) / willingly (bereitwillig)
to be determined to do s. th.
to reject s. th.
to be loath (abgeneigt) / **be reluctant** (widerstrebend) / be disinclined (abgeneigt) / **refuse** (s. weigern) **to do s. th.**
an action is voluntary (done without compulsion) – (freiwillig) / **involuntary** (done with compulsion or done to a person)
to do s. th. voluntarily / involuntarily

capacity – (Auffassungsgabe, geistige Fähigkeit)

a person has / **possesses the capacity to** think / remember / imagine / will . . . s. th.

ability (abilities)

word field: **ability** / **skill** / **competence** (for – Befähigung, Tauglichkeit) / **effeciency** (Tüchtigkeit, Leistungsfähigkeit)

defining phrases: ability, in the singular, denotes a person's physical or mental power to act in a certain way (Fähigkeit); ***abilities,*** in the plural, refers to a person's current level of achievement (augenblicklicher Leistungsstand) (geistige Befähigung, Fähigkeiten)

word family: **ability** / **disability** (Unvermögen, Unfähigkeit) – **to be able** / **unable to do s. th.** – able (fähig) adj. / unable adj.

use (field of collocation):
to have the ability to do s. th. / learn s. th.
to have an ability for . . . (a particular / an administrative job)
to test / assess **a person's mental abilities** / vocational abilities (beruflich)
to be an *able* (fähig, tüchtig) / *unable* statesman / orator . . .

aptitude – (Begabung, Auffassungsgabe, Eignung)

to have an aptitude for . . . (mathematics / languages / mechanics . . .)
to be apt (begabt, geschickt) / **inapt at doing s. th.**

Trait

word field: **trait** / idiosyncrasy (geistige Eigenart) / **characteristic** / feature (Haupteigenschaft, Grundzug) – **habit** – **attitude** / **view** / sentiment / **opinion** – **outlook** / conception / **concept** – **behaviour** / **conduct** / **manner** / air / **manners** / tact / decency / propriety / demeanour / mannerism

trait [trei]

denotes a permanent individual characteristic in a person's behaviour (Charakterzug)

a person has / distinguishes himself from others by **specific traits**
to characterize s. o. by a number of traits / traits of character

some dominant traits in persons
a(n) intelligent / dull – practical / imaginative – industrious / lazy – conscientious / superficial – mature / emotional (gefühlsbetont, -bestimmt) – liberal / conservative person

a(n) kind / aloof (zurückhaltend) – trusting / suspicious (mißtrauisch) – sociable (gesellig) / withdrawn – reliable / unreliable – generous / selfish – grateful / ungrateful person

a(n) active / passive – shamefaced (verschämt) / shameless (schamlos) – assertive (anmaßend) / timid – tough / sensitive – brave / cowardly person

Habit

word field: **habit** / routine / rut (alter Trott)

habit – (Gewohnheit, Angewohnheit)

to get into a habit / a routine / a rut (in e. gleichbleibenden Trott verfallen)
to get into the habit of doing s. th.
s. th. becomes / is a habit
to be in the habit of . . . (doing s. th.) / be in a rut (stagnieren)

View

word field: **attitude** / position (Standpunkt, Haltung) / **view** / sentiment / **opinion** / **outlook** / conception / **concept** / construct (['– –] – gedankliche Konstruktion)

attitude

denotes the relatively stable way an individual feels and behaves towards s. o. (Haltung, Einstellung, Gesinnung)
to have / take / assume / adopt / display **an attitude towards s. o. / to s. th.**
to maintain (beibehalten) / **change** / undermine (untergraben) an attitude

view – (Ansicht, Auffassung)

a person takes (vertreten) **/ holds / has a view of / on s. th.**
he takes the view that . . .
he holds a favourable / poor view of s. o.'s behaviour / performance (Leistung)
in my view (meiner Ansicht nach)
he takes / adopts / has / defends a point of view / viewpoint (Standpunkt)

he speaks / judges **from a point of view / from the point of view of** . . . (the insider . . .)

opinion

denotes a general and subjective view formed or held temporarily (zeitweilig) on a particular question (Meinung)
to form / hold an opinion about s. th. / of s. o. / on a question
to be of the opinion that . . .
in / to my opinion (meiner Meinung nach)
to have an *opinion poll* ([pəul] – Meinungsumfrage) on a public issue
to study / estimate / assess *public opinion* on

*

outlook

denotes a person's habitual (gewohnheitsmäßig) way of looking at things (Einstellung, Weltanschauung)
a person has **a personal outlook on life**
he has a narrow / limited / constricted / infantile / **broad outlook (on life)**
he has a (stable) **moral / religious / ethical outlook**
his general outlook is working class / middle class . . .

concept
denotes *the product of a process* of abstraction (Vorstellung, Begriff)
to have a(n) clear / exact / distinct (deutlich) – **vague / confused / false concept of s. th.**
to conceive s. th. (sich vorstellen) / the idea of things never seen

BEHAVIOUR

word field: **behaviour / conduct / manner** / air / **manners** / tact / decency / propriety / demeanour / mannerism

behaviour – (Verhalten, Benehmen)

to have / show / display (**good / bad** / harsh / **polite / impolite** . . .) **behaviour towards . . .**
to model one's behaviour on s. o. (s. zum Vorbild nehmen)
to observe / watch over / disapprove / **condemn s. o.'s behaviour**
to find fault with s. o.'s behaviour
to praise (loben) – reprehend (tadeln) / blame (ds.) / **criticize / reproach / reprove** (rügen) / **rebuke** (zurechtweisen, e. scharfen Verweis erteilen) / reprimand (maßregeln) **s. o. for his behaviour**
to observe rules / precepts / guides / **codes of behaviour**
to behave / misbehave in a situation
to behave with politeness / civility (Artigkeit) / **courtesy . . .**

manner
is a person's characteristic way of behaving towards others (Art, Betragen, Auftreten)
a person has a(n) strange / offhand (lässig) / abrupt / frigid (frostig) / curt (barsch) / **impolite / gruff** (schroff) / **blunt** (schonungslos, offen) / commanding / peremptory (gebieterisch) / imperious (ds.) / **boisterous** (stürmisch, laut) / **flashy** (protzig) / **pleasing** / bland (einschmeichelnd) / easy / **gentle / suave** ([swɑːv] – verbindlich, zuvorkommend) **manner**
he is strange . . . in his manner

manners
together form the habitual style of one's behaviour in social intercourse (gesellschaftlicher Verkehr) – (Umgangsformen)
a person learns / acquires / has (good / refined [fein] / **bad** / approved / execrable [abscheulich] . . .) **manners**
to be polite / coarse (grob) . . . **in one's manners**
it is good / bad manners to do s. th. (es gehört sich / . . . nicht)

tact
denotes the ability to understand / respect and adjust oneself to (s. anpassen an) the feelings and views of others (Takt, Feingefühl)
to have / possess / behave with / show tact towards s. o. / in a situation / in dealing with others
to treat s. o. with tact
to be tactful / do s. th. tactfully
to show *tactfulness*
to be tactless / gauche ([gəuʃ] – taktlos, linkisch)

Character

| *word field:* **character / disposition / temperament / nature / type**

character

defining phrases: the term is used with reference to the integration of outlook, habits, traits and sentiments which makes an individual's actions relatively stable and predictable (vorhersagbar) – (Charakter)

word family: **character / characterization / characteristics** / characterology / **to characterize s. o. / to be characteristic of**

use (field of collocation):
some action / behaviour is in / out of character with a person's usual behaviour (paßt / paßt nicht zu . . .)
it is in keeping with s. o.'s character (im Einklang mit)
a person's character is formed / determined / influenced by heredity (Vererbung) / **environment** (Umwelt)

to study the development of a person's character / differences in character
s. o. has a good / bad / strange character
he has a strong / dynamic / weak character

Typology

typology [taiˈpɔlədʒi]
denotes the study of the possible classification of human beings according to constitutional make-up / attitude / habitual response, etc. (Typologie)
according to the classical *typology of temperaments* (still partly alive in everyday speech) a person may be called **a sanguine** (amiable, habitually hopeful and pleasant person) / **phlegmatic** (habitually slow and listless [teilnahmslos] person) / **choleric** (easily excited and temperamental person) / **melancholic** (habitually depressed person) **person**
s. th. (behaviour . . .) **is typical of . . .**
to *typify* s. th. (verkörpern, e. typisches Beispiel für)

types according to everyday language
everyday language distinguishes numerous types by listing extreme deviations (Abweichungen) from the normal person / by emphasizing some dominant trait / attitude / way of behaviour in a person

differences in outlook
a person is an optimist / enthusiast / devotee (eifriger Anhänger) / **believer / puritan** / aesthete
he is a pessimist / sceptic / hypochondriac (Schwermütiger, Hypochonder) / agnostic / **atheist** / man-hater / woman-hater (Weiberfeind) / **cynic** (bitterer Spötter)

differences in intelligence and knowledge
a person is a(n) thinker / philosopher / intellectual / highbrow (Intellektueller) / **know-all** (Besserwisser, Schlaumeier) / bookworm / blue-stocking / dreamer
he is a(n) lowbrow (geistig Anspruchsloser) / **ignoramus** ([ˈrei] – Nichtskönner) / dope (Trottel) / **dullard** (Dummkopf) / greenhorn (Grünschnabel) / **fool / clown** / crank (komischer Kauz) / **freak** (unberechenbarer, verrückter Kerl) / **lunatic** (Irrer) / imbecile ([ˈimbisiːl] – Schwachsinniger) / **idiot / madman** (Verrückter)

differences in generosity
a person is a(n) altruist / **philanthropist / humanitarian** (Menschenfreund)
he is a(n) egoist / miser (Geizhals) / cut-throat (Halsabschneider) / misanthrope ([ˈmizənθrəup] – Menschenfeind)

differences in group dominance
a person is a loner (Einzelgänger) / **shirker** (Drückeberger) / **coward** (Feigling)
he is a bully (Schikanierer) / **braggart** (Aufschneider) / swaggerer (Prahler, Großtuer) / **boaster** (Prahler) / megalomaniac (Größenwahnsinniger)
differences in task solving
a person is a worker / **swot** (Streber) / **plodder** (Arbeitstier) / drudge (Arbeitstier, Packesel, Aschenbrödel) / busy-body (Übereifriger) / **pedant**
he is a(n) idler (Müßiggänger) / lazybones / sluggard (Faulpelz) / **tramp** / bum (Stromer) / hippy

(ix) *Visible action*

word field: **action** / **act** / plot / **deed** – feat / exploit / **activity** / doings (manœuvres / tactics) / **occupation** – **performance** / **accomplishment** / **achievement**

action – (Handlung)

word family: **to act** / **be active** / **inactive** / **action** / **act** / **actor** (1. Schauspieler; 2. Handelnder)
use (field of collocation):
to take action for / **against s. th.**
to consider / **plan** / contemplate / premeditate / **choose a course of action**
to perform / **carry through** / **carry out an action**
a person does / **performs** / **commits** (negative implications) **s. th.**
he acts in a certain way / from certain motives
he starts / **begins** / **exploits** (ausnutzen) / **accomplishes** / **achieves** / **completes** / **finishes** / **terminates** / **ends** / **stops s. th.**
he acts under duress ([djuəˈres] – unter Zwang) / **stress** / **strain**
he acts in haste / **panic** / **a characteristic way**
he counteracts the plans of others
he is the actor / **the victim** (Opfer, Leidtragender)
act – ([einzelne] Tat)
to commit an act of ... (folly / injustice / violence [Gewalttätigkeit] / cruelty ...)
deed
denotes s. th. conspicuous (auffallend), done with intention and accomplished (bedeutende Tat; böse Tat)
to do / **perform a deed of** ... (daring ...)
to do a(n) good / **brave** / **heroic deed**
to commit / charge s. o. with an **evil deed**

*

activity
refers to the doing of, and occupation with, a number of things (Tätigkeit, Beschäftigung)
to engage in / occupy oneself with an activity
to engage in **useful** / **outdoor** (in freier Luft) / recreational (Freizeitbeschäftigung) / numerous ... **activities**

performance
denotes either the dealing with and execution of s. th. promised or ordered (Ausführung) or s. th. accomplished / achieved (Leistung)
to perform an action / a task

accomplishment
denotes the completion (Vollendung), especially that of s. th. difficult (Ausführung, Vollendung, Leistung)
s. th. is an **accomplishment**
to accomplish s. th. / nothing

achievement
denotes the performance of some difficult, but worthwhile exploit (Leistung, Großtat)
s. th. is an achievement
to achieve a(n) goal / end / objective
to achieve success / a victory

(x) *The individual in groups*

he is alone / by himself / keeps himself aloof (s. fernhalten) **from others**
he seeks out the company of / establishes contact with / **contacts** ([–'–] – s. in Verbindung setzen mit) / **makes friends with / is friends with others**
he lives together with / has relations with (other people) – (Kontakte, Beziehungen zu) / **a relationship to** or with (another person) – (Beziehung zu) / encounters (Begegnungen) with others

some basic interpersonal behaviour patterns
1. acceptance – respect – admiration – trust – honesty – agreement – help – friendship – praise
a person ACCEPTS / **acknowledges** (anerkennen) / RESPECTS / esteems (schätzen) / **honours** / ADMIRES / adores (verehren, tief bewundern) / idolizes / **worships** / TRUSTS / puts trust in / confides in / has faith in / **relies on** / consults (um Rat angehen) / **is** FRANK with / outspoken with / **sincere** with / candid (aufrichtig) **with** / AGREES **with** / complies with (befolgen) / concurs with (übereinstimmen mit) / **consents to** / concedes s. th. to (zugestehen) ... **(another person / s. o.'s statements)**

he HELPS / **supports** / **backs** (stützen, eintreten für) / assists / **advises** / **teaches** / assures (s. o. of s. th. – e. Sache versichern) / **encourages** (ermutigen) / **warns** / rehabilitates / consoles (trösten) / BEFRIENDS (s. j-s annehmen) / pacifies / soothes (beruhigen) / **reconciles himself with** (s. versöhnen mit) / PRAISES / exalts (verherrlichen) / **flatters** (schmeicheln) / **cajoles** (s. o. into doing s. th. – schmeicheln, verleiten zu) . . . **another person**

2. rejection – disrespect – contempt – mistrust – insincerity – disagreement – desertion – quarrel – reproof

a person REJECTS (ablehnen) / **avoids** (vermeiden) / **ignores** (nicht beachten) / DISRESPECTS (nicht achten) / **dishonours** (schimpflich behandeln) / DESPISES (verachten) / **looks down on** / scorns (geringschätzen) / **kids** (foppen) / **teases** (hänseln) / hoaxes (anführen, zum besten haben) / scoffs at (spotten über) / **mocks** (ds.) / derides (verhöhnen) / jeers at (spotten über) / **insults** (beleidigen) / **condemns** (verurteilen) / MISTRUSTS / has no faith in / **is** INSINCERE **with** (unaufrichtig) / **betrays** (verraten) / **lies to** / **cheats** (betrügen) / beguiles (s. o. into doing s. th. – täuschen) / **deceives** (irreführen, hintergehen) / **bluffs** / **tricks (s. o. into doing s. th.** – überlisten) / DISAGREES **with** / **contradicts** (widersprechen) / **opposes** (entgegentreten) / confronts (feindlich gegenübertreten) / dissents from (anderer Meinung sein) / **defies** (trotzen, s. widersetzen) / **disobeys** (nicht gehorchen) / **challenges** (herausfordern) / is at variance with (Streit haben) / **has a row** (Streit, Krach haben) **with another person**

he DESERTS (im Stich lassen) / forsakes / **leaves** (s. o. in the lurch) / FIGHTS **with** / **quarrels with** / **nags at** (herumnörgeln an) / incriminates (beschuldigen, belasten) / **accuses** / **indicts** (anklagen) / REPROVES (tadeln) / **reproaches** / **blames** (die Schuld geben) / reprimands (maßregeln) / **chides** (schelten) / scolds (ausschelten) / defames (verleumden) / **slanders** (verleumden) / denounces (öffentlich anprangern) / maligns (beschimpfen) **another person**

3. superiority – inferiority

a person COMMANDS (j-m gebieten) / **demands s. th. from** (fordern) / **orders** / **pushes** (antreiben) / **oppresses** / maltreats (schlecht behandeln) / **punishes** (bestrafen) **another person**

he receives deference (Achtung) . . . from others

he SUBMITS **to** (s. unterwerfen) / is devoted to (ergeben) / **is deferential to** (ehrerbietig) / is subservient to (unterwürfig) **another person**

he appeals to s. o. (appellieren an) / **asks s. o. for s. th.** (bitten um) / **begs for** (demütig bitten) / **requests s. o. to do s. th.** (ersuchen, höflich bitten) / solicits s. o. for (angehen um) / **entreats s. o.** (eindringlich bitten) / beseeches s. o. (flehentlich bitten) / **implores s. o.** (beschwören, flehentlich bitten) / supplicates s. o. for (erflehen, demütig bitten um)

(3) Analysis

word field: **criticism** / **analysis** / **interpretation** – scrutiny / examination / **study** / investigation – **comment** / commentary / gloss – **review** / appreciation / **evaluation** – exegesis / **elucidation** / explication / **explanation** / exposition / **paraphrase** / **summary**

terms which apply to the various aspects of criticism collectively

criticism

defining phrases: criticism, in this context, is a general term for aspects of the activity of analyzing, explaining and discussing a literary text (Interpretation, kritische Untersuchung)

word family: **criticism** / **the critic** / **to criticize s. th.** (kritisieren) / **critical** / a criterion, -ia (Kriterium) / a critique

use (field of collocation):
to give / **write** / **present a criticism of a literary text**

the accomplishment of criticism
criticism shows / **discusses** / exposes (enthüllen, darlegen) / **reveals** / **elucidates** (erhellen) / **comments on** / **explains** / **interprets** / **reviews** (besprechen, rezensieren) / appreciates (würdigen) / **evaluates** (werten) / **judges** / passes judgment on **the meaning of a text**

kinds of criticism
a critic gives a general / **summary** / **close** (genau) / penetrating / **thorough** (gründlich) **criticism of a text**
he specializes in **biographical** / **historical** / **genre** (Gattungs-) / **philosophical** / **literary** / **textual criticism**
a critic follows the moral / **psychological** / **sociological** / **formalistic** / **structuralistic** / **archetypal** / **linguistic approach to a text**
he is aware of the principles of **literary history** / **literary criticism** / **philology** / **poetics** / **stylistics** – **of the author's biography** / **the genesis** (Entstehungsgeschichte) **of a text**
a critic employs / **follows a** scheme / **technique** / **mode** / **system of criticism** – –

he *criticizes* (besprechen, rezensieren) a work of art / text
he follows a **critical** approach
he judges / analyzes by certain *criteria*
he uses / employs s. th. as a *criterion* of . . .
he expresses criticism of s. th. (Kritik äußern an)

analysis

defining phrases: the term denotes a kind of criticism that examines the component parts of a text and elucidates (erhellen, erläutern) their structural interrelationship (Wechselbeziehung) – (Deutung, Analyse)

word family: **analysis, -es / to analyze s. th. / an analyst / analytic(al)**

use (field of collocation):

to give / make / write / present / submit (vorlegen) **/ set out on /** embark on **an analysis of a literary text**

to give an analysis of the composition / structure / morphological build-up / divisions / parts / sections / subdivisions / units of meaning of a text

to give an analysis of dominant leads (Hauptlinien) / threads of a theme

to give a critical / close / thorough / penetrating / **subtle analysis of . . .** (aspects of a text)

to give a linguistic / stylistic / verbal / **structural analysis of**

to give a summary / superficial analysis of

interpretation – (Auslegung, Deutung, Interpretation)

to give / present **/ make . . . an interpretation of a text**

an interpretation shows / explains / expounds (auslegen) **/ elucidates . . . the meaning of a text**

to give a misinterpretation of a text

to interpret / misinterpret a text

criticism with an emphasis on thoroughness

examination

denotes an intense look at details of a text (Untersuchung)

close **examination reveals / shows** that

to examine a passage . . .

study – (wissenschaftliche Untersuchung, Studie)

to write / make a study of a literary text

a text requires close / careful . . . study of its elements

criticism with an emphasis on partial explanation

comment

denotes a more or less personal / subjective statement on some particular aspect of a text (Stellungnahme, Anmerkung)

to give / present / deliver / furnish / **make an illuminating comment on** a text

to comment on a theme / phrase . . .

evaluation – (Wertung, Beurteilung)
to give / write an evaluation of
to evaluate a work of art

criticism with an emphasis on general explanation

explanation – (Erklärung, Auslegung)
to give / put forth / offer **an explanation of**
to explain a text
paraphrase [ˈpærəfreiz]
is the restatement (wiederholende Darstellung) of the meaning of a text in other and simpler words (Umschreibung, Paraphrase)
to give a paraphrase of
to paraphrase a text

summary – (Zusammenfassung)
to give a summary of . . . (a novel . . .)
to give a summary (zusammenfassend) **explanation of**
to sum up the contents of . . .

II. THE SPEAKER

the term *speaker* is used with reference to the role / mask / character into which the author projects his outlook on the world (der Sprecher)

the speaker assumes a role / mask / voice
he speaks through a *persona* (mask)
he assumes a traditional role – the role of the story-teller (first-person) **/ narrator** (Erzähler) **/ observer / onlooker**
he is the lyrical / dramatic / poetic I (das lyrische . . . Ich) **of a text**

the speaker views things from a particular angle
he has a point of view (Blickwinkel, Erzählerstandpunkt) **/ viewpoint** / perspective
he has a(n) omniscient / semi-omniscient / limited point of view

he speaks in a tone – a(n) detached / **ironic** / playful / **humorous . . . tone**
the speaker states / asks / claims / maintains / suggests / hints at / implies . . . s. th. (cf. word, p. 75)

III. COMPOSITION AND STRUCTURE

1. The organization of thought

word field: **organization** / **structure** / architecture / **frame** / construction – **form** / **composition** / **shape** / mould / **arrangement** / scheme / **order** / plan / outline / design – **pattern** / fabric / **texture** / tissue

organization

refers to the peculiar, meaningful arrangement and interrelation (Wechselbeziehung) of words, sentences and ideas in a literary text (Gestaltung, Gliederung, systematischer Aufbau)
a literary text has / possesses / contains / shows a particular organization of its elements
the organization of a text controls / orders / shapes the meaning
a text has **a(n) simple / complex** / intricate (verwickelt) / balanced **organization**

structure

defining phrases: the term is used with reference to the organization of linguistic elements in a literary text. It emphasizes the build-up and interrelation of units of meaning – (Bau, Gefüge, Struktur)
word family: **structure** / superstructure / **structural** / **structuralistic** / **structured** (strukturiert)
use (field of collocation):
a literary text has / possesses / contains / shows a structure
the structure of a text controls / order / shapes / determines the **meaning / the relation of the parts to the whole**
a text has a(n) simple / complex / intricate / interwoven (verflochten) **structure**
elements of the structure of a text are parts / divisions / sections ...
(cf. composition: compositional elements, p. 47)

*

form

is a term (now) regarded as loose and ambiguous (doppeldeutig) if applied to the organization and structure of a text. *Form* refers to the (visible) order imposed on a text rather than to the order rising

from a poetic or literary utterance itself (though some critics speak of the "inner form" of a text). Hence its main application nowadays is with the more or less clearly defined *poetic forms* (genres) such as the sonnet / ode ... (Form)
to impose / superimpose a form on a literary text
to choose / create a (new) form for a poetic utterance
to write a poem in the form of ... (a sonnet ...)

composition

refers to the arrangement of units of meaning of a text. The term implies a loose reference to the interrelation of the parts (Aufbau, Zusammensetzung, Komposition)
a text has a composition
the composition of a text orders / allocates (den Platz bestimmen) **units of meaning and individual elements**
a text has a symmetrical / framed / ring ... composition
to study compositional elements / analogies / **parallels / contrasts / antitheses**
COMPOSITIONAL ELEMENTS OF A TEXT **are the whole / parts / divisions / sections / subdivisions / groups of lines** / (narrative or pictorial) **units of meaning / paragraphs – acts / scenes / chapters / stanzas**
a text divides naturally / falls / breaks down into (a number of) **parts** / divisions / sections

*

arrangement

refers to the planned order in which the poet places and presents his words and sentences (Anordnung, Zusammenstellung)
words / sentences / stanzas ... follow one another in a particular arrangement
to arrange s. th. in a certain order / in a semblance (Anschein) of order
to rearrange the succession of thoughts

order – (Ordnung, Reihenfolge)

words are placed / set / arranged / appear in a certain order – in alphabetical / in an unusual order / in order of ascending (descending) importance
elements of a sentence / paragraph are arranged in an ascending order (i. e. climactically) / a descending order (i. e. anticlimactically) / the order of cause and effect / the order of inductive (deductive) reasoning

to introduce order / a climactic order (auf e. Höhepunkt gerichtet) in a text / **among its elements**
to study the order of words / parts of a sentence / sentences
to find an order of increasing concreteness / specification / generalization / abstraction in a text
order establishes relationships among words

outline
denotes the plan of a composition, written out in a series of numbered headings (Gliederung, Überblick)
to make / draw up / write out an outline
a(n) brief / preliminary / explicit outline
a topic (Überschriften-) / sentence outline

*

pattern – (Muster, Anlage)
a sentence / stanza / poem / short story has / shows a pattern
elements / parts . . . of a text **form / create** / establish **a pattern**
rhythms follow / establish patterns

2. Stages in the succession of thoughts

THE WHOLE (das Ganze)
to develop a(n) thought / idea / conception / opinion / **standpoint** / position . . .
to move a thought through a paragraph / from a beginning through a middle to an end
to follow a(n) new / unusual train / line . . . of thought
to contemplate / consider / meditate on / argue a case
a text has a subject / theme / topic
it has a(n) succession / series / sequence (Folge) / (dialectical) coordination / subordination / **interrelation** (Wechselbeziehung) / **transitions** (Überleitung) **of thoughts**

SUBJECT / THEME (Thema)
s. th. is the subject / theme / principal thought / main line of argument **of a text**
to say s. th. about / treat / treat of / deal with / be concerned with / tackle (angreifen) / **develop a subject / theme (in detail / at some length . . .)**
to speak about **the subject-matter** (thought content) – (Gegenstand, Stoff) **of a text**

*

THE THESIS (These)
the thought of a text is developed in the stages of thesis / antithesis / synthesis . . .

the author puts forth / puts forward / presents / develops / elaborates / defends / attacks a thesis / the thesis that ...
to present the *antithesis* / *synthesis* of / to s. th.
an argument is the (very) **antithesis of / to another**

the exposition (Darlegung)
to explain a(n) theme / subject / idea **in detailed exposition**

the argument ([Beweis]Grund, Argument)
to use / put forward / advance (vorbringen) **an argument for / against s. th.**
to support / corroborate (erhärten) **an argument**
to base / ground one's arguments / counter-arguments **on (facts ...)**
to disprove / confute (widerlegen) / refute (ds.) **an argument**
to argue (argumentieren) coherently / consistently (folgerichtig) / **conclusively** (schlüssig) / incoherently / inconsistently / **inconclusively**

a reason (Grund)
to give / put forward / advance a reason for / against
to support / justify / **disprove ... an argument by (strong / convincing ...) reasons**
to give **good** / sound / strong / **convincing** / decisive / **feeble / weak reasons for / against s. th.**

a condition (Bedingung)
to set / make s. th. / pose (aufstellen) **a condition for**
a(n) main / principal / subsidiary / additional condition

*

the proof (Beweis)
to give / ... produce / raise arguments in proof of s. th.
to give proof of s. th. / that s. th. is the case
an argument stands proof / does not stand (much) proof

an example (Beispiel)
to seek for / search for / **find / give / draw upon** (zurückgreifen auf) / **quote** / cite / adduce / **refer to an example** (from)
an example demonstrates / illustrates / illuminates / amplifies (näher ausführen) / clarifies / specifies an idea / **abstraction through concrete detail**
to give **a(n) concrete / illustrative / fitting** (passend) / appropriate (angemessen, passend) **example**
to say s. th. by way of (als) example
here are some (more) examples for
for example (= for instance, e. g. = exempli gratia – zum Beispiel)
to exemplify s. th. by ... (a quotation / quoting from ...)

a quotation (Zitat, Textstelle, Beleg)
to give / put in / insert (einfügen) **/ take a quotation from . . .** (a text / an author . . .)
to place a quotation in / tear a quotation from its (proper) **context**
to quote a sentence / passage from (anführen, zitieren)
to quote in (im [Sinn]Zusammenhang) **/ out of context**
to quote literally (wörtlich) / generally / extensively from
to *cite* (zitieren, s. berufen auf) an example / authority (by quoting from . . .)
to cite a source / X (some name) as (an expert on . . .) . . .

a *citation,* in this context, is the source / reference of a quoted statement (Anführung, Zitat)
to give a footnote / identifying citation at the end of a quotation

*

THE ANTITHESIS
to present the antithesis of s. th.
s. th. is / forms the antithesis to the preceding argument
an antithesis is expressed in . . . (a line / paragraph . . .)

an objection (Einwand)
to put forward / advance / raise / make . . . an objection to an argument
to object (Einwände erheben) by pointing out a contradiction (Widerspruch) / an inconsistency in an argument

a contrast (['kɔntrɑːst] – Gegensatz)
to present / form / offer **/ produce a contrast to s. th.**
to find a **slight** / light / **strong** / striking / **subtle** / profound **contrast**
s. th. contrasts (finely / grossly [grob] / coarsely . . .) **with**

*

a comparison (Vergleich) – (also cf. VIII. style)
to draw / make / resort to a comparison between . . . and . . .
s. th. bears / stands comparison with (den Vergleich aushalten)
in comparison with (im Vergleich zu) s. th. / an argument is . . .
to compare s. th. with an object (of the same class) / to (an object of a different class)
to compare things at (great) **length / in detail**
an object compares well (s. vergleichen lassen) / favourably / **cannot compare with s. th. else**
to compare an adjective (steigern)

a distinction (Unterschied, Unterscheidung)
to make / draw / arrive at / formulate **a distinction**
to make (nice [genau] / **subtle** / coarse ...) **distinctions between**
to distinguish between ... and ... / s. th. from s. th. else

a definition (Definition, [Begriffs]Bestimmung)
to give / find / form / frame / arrive at **a definition of** ... (a term / word ...)
to give **a(n) clear / exact / precise / correct / wrong** / false / insufficient / **incomplete definition of**
to define a term

*

THE SYNTHESIS
to give / present / come to the synthesis of ... (what has been analyzed)

consequence (Folge, [Schluß]Folgerung)
an argument comes as / is / follows as a consequence of
s. th. is of no (belanglos) / **of consequence for**
s. th. has (serious / grave ...) **consequences**

a transition ([træn'siʒən] – Überleitung, Übergang)
the speaker **provides** the reader with **a transition from ... to ...**
he passes / moves from one idea to another by a transition
there is a transition from ... to ...
the speaker uses a **transitional** sentence / paragraph
he moves to s. th. else (übergehen zu)

THE CONCLUSION (Schluß, Schlußfolgerung)
to draw / lead up to / proceed towards / **come to / arrive at / reach / jump to (at** – voreilig ziehen) **a conclusion** (from)
s. th. brings an argument to / forms / is a conclusion
to conclude / end / close / finish / tie off / **terminate** (beenden) **a speech with**
to conclude / gather (schließen) / **infer** / deduce **s. th. from**
an argument is conclusive / inconclusive

the solution (Lösung)
to seek / **find** / discover / **arrive at a solution / the solution to / of / for a problem**

IV. THE LITERARY GENRES

(1) Fiction

word field: **literature** / **fiction** / invention / **fantasy**

fiction

defining phrase: the term *fiction* is used with reference to prose narratives (novels / short stories, etc.) – (Prosaerzählungen) which present something invented or imagined ([Prosa]Dichtung)

word family: **fiction** / **fictitious** (not real, s. th. imagined, made up, invented) – (erfunden, vorgetäuscht) / **fictional** (relating to the art of fiction) / fictive (fiktiv, erdichtet)

use (field of collocation):

to read / **write fiction**

to analyze **a work of fiction**

the main genres of fiction are the novel / **epic** / romance / **short story** / **detective story** / **tale** / novelette (novella) / **anecdote** / fable / parable / **myth** / saga / legend

to read **a story of science** / utopian / **popular (commercial) fiction**

to prefer **non-fiction** to fiction

novel

word field: **novel** / **(prose) narrative** (Erzählung) / **story** / **(adventure** / **spy** / **crime** / ghost- . . . **story)** / **work of fiction** / **fiction** / **tale** / romance

defining phrases: a *novel* **is** a long prose narrative about fictitious persons and a number of fictitious events (Roman)

word family: **novel** / **novelist** / novelistic / novelette (novella)

use (field of collocation):

types of novel

basic types of the novel are the novel of action / **novel of character** / **dramatic novel**

other types are the **historical** / period / political / **sociological** / propagandist **novel** – the novel of social criticism

other types are **the adventure** / **picaresque** (Schelmen-) **novel** – **the autobiographical** (fictitious memoirs of . . .) / **biographical** / **epistolary** [iˈpistələri] novel (told in letters) / psychological **novel** – **the künstlerroman** (novel about an artist) / **bildungsroman** (novel of educational formation / novel of development)

popular present-day forms of the novel are crime stories / detective fiction / science fiction – –

a novelist uses a narrative technique – the epistolary / point-of-view / stream-of-consciousness technique

COMPOSITION AND COMPONENT PARTS OF A NOVEL

a novel is composed of several books / parts / divisions / chapters
a CHAPTER **opens with / deals with / tells of / describes . . . reveals** (a theme . . .)
it is subdivided into . . . (paragraphs . . .)
a novel has episodes / digresssions (Abschweifung) **/ themes / motifs / leitmotifs / planes of action / levels of action**

CHIEF ELEMENTS / ingredients (Bestandteil) **of the novel are character / plot** (Fabel) **/ setting** (Hintergrund, Schauplatz, Raum) **/ language**
it is told from a particular point of view / has shiftings (Wechsel) **of viewpoint**

CHARACTER IN A NOVEL

character is / is not the centre of a novel
a novel presents / introduces / delineates / portrays many characters
it presents fictitious (erdacht) **persons / figures**
it explores the psyche / mind / thought / inner workings **/ stream of consciousness /** flow of consciousness **of a character**
a novelist creates / designs **new characters**
he views them from an unusual angle / a particular point of view
he presents them in dialogue / substitutionary narration (erlebte Rede)
a novel has a(n) STORY-TELLER **/ narrator / observer / onlooker**
it has a(n) partial / impartial (unparteiisch) observer – **an observer with a limited / an omniscient point of view**
the author keeps himself out of the story he narrates / enters the mind of a character / speaks through one of his characters / takes a character as his mouthpiece
a novel has flat / round characters
it has types / caricatures [ˌkærikəˈtjuəz]
the author **sets characters in a scene / background**

PLOT IN A NOVEL

a novel has a plot (Fabel) – **it tells of events /** occurrences (Begebenheiten) / happenings **in the form of a plot**
it tells / relates a story
it is based on "a narrative of events arranged in their time sequence" (E. M. Forster's definition of a story), **but places emphasis on causality / on the cause and effect relationship of events**

it presents a "chain of events in a story" (E. Muir)
the author plans a novel
he weaves / **constructs / contrives** (ersinnen) **a plot**
he links / concatenates (verknüpfen) **events**
he contrives a(n) ending / conclusion / dénouement ([dei'nuːmɑ̃ːŋ] – Lösung des Knotens)
a novel unfolds according to an elaborate scheme
it has flashbacks (Rückblenden) / **an episodic structure**
a plot is consistent / inconsistent – coherent / incoherent – **tightly / loosely woven**

SETTING IN A NOVEL

a novel has a setting / locale ([ləu'kɑːl] – Schauplatz) / climate / **atmosphere / period in which the action takes place**
it has a(n) **historical / contemporary** (zeitgenössisch) / **realistic / fantastic setting**

LANGUAGE IN A NOVEL

a novel is written in prose / dialogue
it is told in the first person / third person / past tense
it has descriptive / 'purple' (Glanzstellen) **passages**
it has many passages of introspection / (silent) **monologue** (unspoken soliloquy / *monologue intérieur*)
it has many passages in direct / indirect / reported **speech** / oblique narration (indirekte Erzählung) – **substitutionary narration** (erlebte Rede) / **objective report / author's comment**
the language of a novel creates an atmosphere / a tone
the narrator speaks in a(n) matter-of-fact / ironic / satiric / detached / knowing / naïve / playful / serious / intimate **tone**

detective story – (Kriminalroman)

a detective story / mystery story / **thriller** (Reißer) / whodun(n)it (coll.) **deals with the detection of a crime**
its chief / principal characters are **the professional detective / amateur** ['æmətəː] **detective / private detective**
standard ingredients of detective fiction are the seemingly **unbreakable alibi** ['ælibai] / the logical disclosure (Enthüllung) of an unlikely person as the murderer / ruthless (rücksichtslos) characters / **a close-knit plot / misleading clues** (Schlüssel) **to a probable solution**

science fiction

the term (often abbreviated to SF) refers to stories and novels in which scientific (wissenschaftlich) and pseudo-scientific calculations and reasonings are characteristic of the plot. Science fiction is set in

the future (wissenschaftliche Abenteuergeschichte, Zukunftsroman)
science fiction deals with robots / synthetic people / supermen
it deals with parapsychological phenomena / **things that have not yet happened** / **space** (interplanetary) **travel** (Raumfahrt) / **invasions from space** / future wars / future societies / stunning inventions

popular / commercial fiction

as opposed to serious (good) fiction, the term refers to stories and novels with no artistic pretensions (künstlerische Ansprüche). Popular fiction has stereotyped characters / situations / themes / devices, which are intended to satisfy the reader's expectations / desires / drives. They make no particular demands upon his reading capacity (Trivial-, Unterhaltungsliteratur). In their lowest forms, they appeal to the reader's lowest instincts (trashy literature – Schundliteratur)
a much-debated form of trashy literature is the pornographic story / novel
to read trash (Schund) / pulp fiction (ds.) / **a cheap sensational novel** (Sensationsroman) / **sensational story** / penny dreadful (sl.) / shilling shocker / Wild West story / Western (story of cowboy or frontier life in the historical American West)

*

short story

a *short story* is a fictitious narrative in prose shorter and less complex than the novel. It centres around one incident (Begebenheit) in the lives of a limited number of characters, which is often revealed as an unusual incident (kurze Geschichte, englisch-amerikanische Kurzgeschichte)
a short story deals with / concentrates on a limited number of characters
it organizes character and action into a simple plot
it presents / reveals aspects of characters at some single moment of crisis
it presents the encounter / clash of characters
it focuses on the significant incident / **a single turning-point** (Wendepunkt) / **surprising reversal** (Umkehr, Umschwung) **from which the action develops in a(n) new / unforeseen direction**
a short story is often confined to one setting / place / locale / spot
it covers in detail only a short period of time
it is told in language highly charged with meaning / implication / suggestion
the meaning of a short story may be enhanced by the repetition of key words and phrases / leitmotifs

a short story builds up / creates / evokes **dramatic expectation / suspense towards the end / the dénouement** [dei'nu:mã:ŋ]
it may have a frame / be framed / have an abrupt opening / have an abrupt ending
to read **a short / long short story**
a short story writer

anecdote ['ænikdəut]

denotes a simple, usually amusing narration of an incident connected with some person (Anekdote)
to tell / write / hear an anecdote about a person

a joke, in the present context, denotes an anecdote or *witticism* (witzige Bemerkung) which makes one laugh (Witz)
to make / crack a joke

(2) Drama

word field: **drama / play / tragedy /** melodrama / **comedy /** tragicomedy / burlesque / **farce**

drama (play)

defining phrases: the term *drama* refers to the literary form that is designed for the theatre. Drama is the representation (Darstellung) / imitation (Nachahmung) / enactment (Aufführung) / performance of some action
Drama is both action represented and action seen

word family: **drama** [ɑ:] / **dramatic / dramatist** ['dræmətist] / dramatize / dramatization / dramatics

use (field of collocation):

types of play
types of play are the tragedy / melodrama / **comedy /** tragicomedy / burlesque / **farce**
a drama may be a mime (Possenspiel) / **pantomime** (Gebärdenspiel, Pantomime) / dumb show (stummes Spiel)
a play may be a(n) religious drama / heroic drama
it is a(n) thesis drama / **drama of ideas /** problem play / **historical drama / documentary drama** (in recent theatre of fact) – (Dokumentarspiel) / experimental drama / **drama of the absurd / epic drama**
it is a one-act play / trilogy / tetralogy
epic drama / theatre "alienates" (verfremden) **known problems in order to create new points of view**
a drama may be a social problem / social thesis play

drama has its origins in ritual / religious celebrations with mask-wearing performers (Darsteller) – –
a play is written in prose / in verse (blank verse ...)
it is **a prose / verse / poetic drama**
it is composed / written by a(n) **author / playwright / dramatist /** script-writer (Drehbuchautor)
a writer *dramatizes* an incident / recent history / historical matter

THEORY OF DRAMA: THE UNITIES AND CATHARSIS [kəˈθɑːsis]

Aristotle / the French classicists / Brecht has (have) produced a theory of tragedy / drama
an author observes / follows the rules of the theory of the three unities
he observes the unities / the unities of time, place, and action
an action takes place in a span of 24 hours or less
it plays in a single place
a drama appeals to the emotions / to reason
it delights and instructs
drama is said to accomplish catharsis of / to purge the emotions of pity and fear
it excites / arouses / evokes **pity and fear**
elements / component parts / ingredients **of drama are plot / action / character / language / atmosphere / representation** (Darstellung) (see below)

tragedy

the term denotes the representation of a serious action which ends unhappily / disastrously (verhängnisvoll) / generally with the death of the principal character(s)
(Trauerspiel, Tragödie)
common types of tragedy are the revenge tragedy (Rache-) – **tragedy of revenge** / blood / **fate / character** – the bourgeois tragedy (bürgerliches T.) / **domestic tragedy** (ds.)
a tragedy deals with characters of high rank / status / position – **lower-class characters**
it presents an action / a conflict / a disaster (Unglück, Katastrophe)

*

comedy

denotes a type of humorous drama that ends happily. Comedy makes the audience laugh at man's foibles (Schwächen) / follies (Torheiten) / vices (Lustspiel, Komödie)
to classify comedies into plays of **high comedy** (with a dominant intellectual appeal) / **low comedy** (with violent and boisterous action)

common types of comedies are the romantic comedy (dealing with lovers in imaginary landscapes) / sentimental comedy – satiric comedy / critical comedy – the comedy of manners / wit / humours
comedy exposes / mocks at / ridicules / derides (verlachen) **human** foibles / **weaknesses** / frailties / follies / **vices**
it evokes / arouses laughter
low comedy / comedy of the roughest kind is slapstick comedy (Klamaukkomödie) / **contains situational comedy** (Situationskomik)
common devices of comedy are stereotyped characters / **types / stock situations** (like the screen scene) / **verbal wit** (Wortwitz)
scenes of comic relief (cf. action) are episodes in a tragedy that temporarily relieve the tragic effect, often deepening the prevailing sense of tragedy afterwards

THE THEME IN DRAMA

a play has / deals with / treats a theme / subject / an issue (Problem, Streitfrage)
it deals with a topical issue (aktuelles Thema) – **contemporary / historical event**

COMPOSITION AND COMPONENT PARTS IN PLAYS

a play has a(n) subject / theme / plot / subplot / action / characters / chorus
it has acts / scenes / stage directions (Bühnenanweisungen) / a prologue / an epilogue / a succession of *tableaux* ([ˈtæbləu] – in epic drama) – (Bilder)
it has a(n) structure / exposition / rising action (steigende Handlung) / **conflict / crisis / climax / turning-point** / reversal / peripety (Peripetie) – **falling action** (fallende Handlung) / **dénouement** [deiˈnuːmɑ̃ːŋ] / **unknotting of the plot** (Lösung des Handlungsknotens) / **catastrophe** [kəˈtæstrəfi] / **unhappy ending**
the turning-point of a play comes in . . . / at . . .
a play is a one-act play – has a three-act / . . . five-act construction
a scene takes place / plays in . . .
a play has many changes of scene (Szenenwechsel)

THE DRAMATIC DIALOGUE **of a scene advances** (vorantreiben) **the action** – indicates the mood / tone / thought / attitude of a character
conventions of dialogue are verse / long speeches / monologues / soliloquies / asides
the dialogue is written in stichomythia ([ˌstikəuˈmiθiə] – one-line alternating speeches) – (Zeilenrede, Stichomythie) / stichomythic verse
to come upon a key scene (Schlüsselszene)

a play has short / extensive STAGE DIRECTIONS
stage directions provide information about entrances / exits / places /

locations / **setting / characters / gestures and movements / facial expressions / a character's moods / silences ...**

a play has AN EXPOSITION
the exposition usually encompasses (umfassen) the first act / scenes ...
it sets the action in motion / provides information about the principal characters / provides an informational background to / for
a play needs much / little exposition

ACTION IN A PLAY
the term action refers to what happens in a play / the term plot refers to the order in which the action of a play happens
the action of a play takes place / occurs in some place / **in the mind of a character**
the action is plotted – poorly / intricately plotted (cf. below: plot)
the sequence of events is directed towards the end / creates suspense for the end
a play has unity of action / a unified action
dramatic action engages characters in encounter / conflict / quarrel / **action and counteraction** (Gegenaktion)

the action of a play is set in motion by the exposition (*act I* in the classical five-act play)
it is propelled forward by an inciting force (erregendes Moment) / events *(act II)*
it rises to / moves to / evolves into / **mounts up to** / precipitates (beschleunigen) **a conflict / crisis ...** *(act III)*
it culminates / crests (gipfeln) **in a turning-point** / a reversal of the hero's fortune / a peripety
the action is interrupted / delayed by a flashback (Rückblende) / retrospect
events precipitate / **introduce** / signal / indicate **the falling action** *(act IV)*
the action / events / incidents of a play move(s) to a catastrophe
it ends (when it is a tragedy) **with / in a catastrophe** *(act V)*
it ends with a deus-ex-machina solution / dénouement

PLOT IN A PLAY
a play has a light / conventional / serious plot
a play has a(n) simple / loose / complex / involved / intricate / **tight plot**
a play has a single / double plot
a play has a plot with a(n) unhappy / happy ending

CHARACTER IN A PLAY
characters in a play constitute **the dramatis personae** [ˈdræmətis pəːˈsəuni]

they are types / individuals
they are flat / round – static / dynamic **characters**
a playwright creates / makes use of types / stock characters **/ flat characters / characters that behave and act to a set / an expected pattern**
a play has MAJOR **/ minor** CHARACTERS
it has a main / chief / principal / leading character
a character is the hero / heroine / protagonist / antagonist (Gegenspieler)
the protagonist is in conflict with / fights / combats (bekämpfen) **the antagonist / opponents / fate**
a play has men / women / boy characters
the spectators follow the rise of A CHARACTER'S FORTUNE (Geschick, Schicksal)
an event / incident brings about / becomes the cause of **the hero's downfall** (Sturz, Untergang) / tragic fall / misfortune [–ˈ – –]
a common flaw in protagonists is hubris ([ˈhjuːbris] or hybris [ˈhaibris]) / pride / overconfidence in their power
a play has / presents characters of high RANK **/ station / estate** – eminent position
a character has a social status / rank
a play presents lower-class / working-class / middle-class / ordinary / mediocre (durchschnittlich) **heroes / heroines**

A CHARACTER SPEAKS **alone / delivers a monologue** (to be overheard by other characters) **/ speaks a soliloquy** (to be overheard by the audience) **/ thinks out loud / makes an aside / whispers an aside / addresses another character in an aside**
he overhears the conversation of others ... (behind a door / screen [Wandschirm] ...)
he is in colloquy with **/ enters into a dialogue with / addresses / exchanges (witty ...) repartees with others**
he delivers a long speech / gives a climax to his speech / delivers a tirade [taiˈreid]
a character plans / plots / performs / carries out an action
he sets up an intrigue / intrigues against others

LANGUAGE IN A PLAY
a play is written in verse / prose
it has passages of lively / elevated / rhetorical ... **dialogue** (cf. VIII. style)
external events are introduced into the dialogue by a messenger's speech
it is cast in everyday / colloquial / learned ... **English** (cf. VII. language)

*

THE PERFORMANCE OF PLAYS

to give a performance of a play
to stage / **produce** / put on the stage / **perform** / **present a play**
a play belongs to the repertory (['repətəri] – Repertoire) **of** / **is rehearsed** (einstudieren, proben) **by an acting company**

THE EFFECT OF PLAYS

drama is said both to delight and instruct
it is said to communicate to the spectator a sense of pity and fear / a thrill of exaltation ([egzɔːl'teiʃən] – Erhebung)
tragedy **accomplishes** / **effects catharsis** / **the purgation of pity and fear**

*

THE THEATRE BUILDING

to go to the theatre
to go to a(n) open-air theatre / classical amphitheatre ['æmfi,θiətə] / court-theatre (Hof-) / **Broadway theatre** / **off-Broadway theatre**
to go to a provincial / **repertory (rep)** / **touring** (Wanderbühne) **theatre**

THE STAGE

a theatre has a stage / raised platform / **front stage** (Vorderbühne) / **rear** (Hinter-) / **backstage** (ds.)
it has a(n) gallery / **balcony** / **upper stage** / **curtained inner stage**
a theatre has a(n) acting area (Spielfläche) / circular performing area (the amphitheatre) / **platform stage** / apron stage
it has a(n) peep-show (Guckkasten-) / peep-hole / picture-frame / **box-set stage**
the (Elizabethan) **platform stage** (or apron stage – Vorbühne) **juts out** (hineinragen, vorspringen) / projects **into** (ds.) **the audience**
the box-set stage has a proscenium arch (Bühnenrahmen) / **proscenium frame**
it has a(n) proscenium opening / **front curtain** / iron curtain / iron safety curtain / **imaginary fourth wall to the audience**
it is boxed in by walls on three sides / set in a frame
the curtain conceals **scenic alterations**
it marks the end of the main episodes of the action
it rises / **falls** – ascends / descends

SCENERY

on the stage there are stage properties / **props** (Requisiten) / furnishings (Möbel) / **decorations**
there are wings (Kulissenflügel) / painted panels or flats (Kulissen) / **designs of settings** (Bühnenentwürfe)
to use / **employ** / **place on the stage bits of scenery** (Bühnenbild)

to shift scenery
props are handled / moved by scene-shifters

LIGHTING
to give directions for the lighting (Beleuchtung) of the theatre / the auditorium illumination
to light / spotlight / floodlight the stage

SOUND EFFECTS
to use / employ / produce sound effects (Geräuschkulisse)

THE ACTOR
actors / actresses play / enact / perform / present / stage a play
they form / belong to / are members of **the cast** (Ensemble, Besetzung) **of a play**
an actor has a minor / major / principal / star part in a play
he plays a part / role / character
the (leading . . .) **parts of a play are taken by . . .**
to cast (mit Rollen besetzen) **a play / a Negro as Othello**
an actor enters / appears on / leaves the stage
he makes his entrance from the left / the right
he makes his exit to the left / to the right

THE AUDIENCE
the audience applauds – boos a performance
it gives a player a big hand / standing ovation

(3) Poetry

word field: **(lyric) poetry / poem / lyric** / song / **verse – ballad** / hymn / **ode** / elegy (dirge / pastoral elegy / pastoral / georgic) / **sonnet** / complaint / epigram / doggerel

the poem

defining phrases: poems collectively are called *poetry.* A poem is a piece of poetry / verbal art
It is a complex organization of rhythmically patterned and individually structured language
It is a medium for expressing feelings / ideas / insights / experiences
word family: **a poet** / poetess – **poetic(al)** / poetic justice / poetic licence (dichterische Freiheit) – **lyric / epic / dramatic poetry** – prose-poetry / **the poetry of nature** (Naturdichtung) / non-poetry
use (field of collocation):
to write / compose / be inspired to the composition of / draft (entwerfen) / **set down a poem**

a poem is written by / composed by / forms part of the works of a poet
to read a poem by / of John Milton
a poem is by John Milton
to read / speak / speak by heart / recite / declaim a poem
to memorize a poem (know a poem by heart)

composition and component parts
a poem has a title / subtitle / prefaced quotation
it is entitled . . . / subtitled . . .
a poem has (a) **theme / subject / subject-matter**
it deals with / treats of / is concerned with / presents s. th.
the theme of a poem is . . . (love / death / a season . . .)

to look at the poem as a whole
a poem has a division – a division into stanzas / parts / sections / verse groups
it is divided into . . . / composed of . . . / contains . . . / comprises (umfassen, enthalten) . . .
to study the individual thought units / pictorial units of meaning (bildliche Bedeutungseinheiten)

to analyze the stanzas / stanzaic patterns
a poem is composed of two-line / three-line . . . stanzas
a stanza is composed of a number of lines / verses
it has a verbal texture / sound pattern / metre / rhythmical pattern / particular syntax / particular choice of words / images / rhymes (cf. VI. prosody)

levels of meaning in a poem
a poem is spoken from a particular point of view – by the poetic I / the lyrical I / a protagonist / **a speaker**
it reflects qualities of the phenomena presented / has aesthetic qualities / **is highly charged with meaning** – is language heightened / concentrated / condensed

a poem creates / produces / evokes / stirs up / **arouses a sense of / an impression of**
a poem conveys (vermitteln) / **communicates /** imparts (mitteilen) **an impression of . . .**
a poem says / suggests / implies that . . .
it has a significance / **meaning /** relevance to (for) . . .
it appeals to / makes an appeal to

tone and style
a poem has a realistic / romantic / elegiac – religious / philosophic / symbolic / allegoric / satiric **tone or style**
it is a realistic / romantic . . . poem (also cf. VIII. style)

types of poem
to use / employ the form of the ballad / hymn / **ode** / elegy / **sonnet** / doggerel ...
to write / compose a ballad ...

a ballad

is a story dramatically told in the form of a song or poem. The term refers to a dramatic narrative poem (Ballade)
there are different types of ballad
there are traditional / popular / folk – literary / art (Kunstballaden) **ballads**
traditional ballads were improvised by some unknown singer / minstrel
a common stanza form of the ballad is the quatrain – a quatrain of alternating four- and three-stress lines / a quatrain of alternating lines of iambic tetrameter and iambic trimeter
the ballad stanza (often) ends with a refrain [riˈfrein] / chorus

an ode

is a secular (weltlich) "song" / long poem of praise with elaborate stanza patterns (Ode)

an *elegy*

is a serious / melancholy / mournfully contemplative / meditative poem – a funeral song (Elegie)
an elegy laments (beklagen) / bewails (betrauern) / mourns the death of s. th. / s. o.

a sonnet

is a fourteen-line poem with conventional demands as to its structure and rhyme scheme (Sonett)
there are different types of sonnet
to read a(n) Italian (Petrarchan) sonnet / a(n) English (Shakespearian, -ean) sonnet
a sonnet consists of / is composed of / is arranged into / can be divided into quatrains (and a couplet) / **tercets**
the Italian sonnet consists of two quatrains and two tercets / an octave and a sestet
the English sonnet consists of three quatrains and a couplet
to write / compose a sonnet in the Italian / English form
a thematically loosely connected series of sonnets is called **a sonnet sequence** (Sonnetzyklus)

some kinds of poetry
light verse
is a kind of playful poetry such as the **limerick** ("There once was a lady of Riga ...") / *clerihew* (a witty, four-line verse with lines of varying length, usually rhyming in pairs). Light verse is also referred to as *nonsense* / **comic** / *curious* **verse**

(4) Non-Fiction

word field: **non-fiction** / didactic literature / **propaganda**

non-fiction

is a term of classification which sets apart (abteilen) works written in ordinary communicative (mitteilend) and informative language (Sachliteratur; bildende, belehrende Literatur) from works (cf. fiction, p. 52) written in heightened connotative language

book-size types of non-fiction
book-size types of non-fiction are **books of fact** (Sachbücher) – **the history** / chronicle / **biography / autobiography / memoirs** / monograph
a **biography** is a person's life-history written by a biographer
to study *biographic* data
an **autobiography** is a person's own account of his life
to read an *autobiographical* account

shorter types of non-fiction
shorter types of non-fiction are the treatise / dissertation / **thesis** / paper (a scholarly essay) – (Aufsatz, Abhandlung, Vortrag) / **essay** / **sermon** / **article**
a **treatise** is a careful deductive study of one particular subject (Abhandlung, Traktat)
to write a treatise on poetry ...

a *dissertation* is a long and formal account of a subject (Abhandlung, Dissertation)

a **thesis,** in this context, denotes a written essay submitted for a university degree (Staatsarbeit, Dissertation)

an **essay** is a short, usually informal prose composition on some aspects of a subject

a *paper,* in this context, is a scholarly essay or lecture (Aufsatz, Abhandlung, Referat)

an **article** is a short, informative prose piece which appears in newspapers, periodicals, magazines
to read the leading article / leader (Leitartikel) / editorial of a newspaper

propaganda [ˌprɔpəˈgændə]
is a term used with reference to pieces of writing which spread doctrines and ideas of the moment. Propaganda may be an aspect of any work of fiction, drama or poetry
the political *pamphlet* is a kind of (non-fictional) propaganda

V. CONTENT AND MEANING

word field: **content** / contents (gist) / **substance** (essence) / **meaning** / **sense** / **moral** / **lesson**

content [ˈkɔntent]
denotes the substance of what is said in a text (Gehalt, Aussage)
a work of art has no content apart from form
form and content in a text are inseparable
to consider the intellectual / ideological / philosophical content of a novel / play ...

contents [ˈkɔntents]
refers to a summary of the details of a text, of what it says (Inhalt)
to give / sum up the contents of
substance
in this context, refers to the chief meaning / the *essence* of a text (das Wesentliche, die Substanz)
there is / is little / is no substance in a text / an argument

*

meaning
refers to what the words of a literary text collectively say and express as linguistic signs (sprachliche Zeichen) in a particular arrangement (Aussage, Bedeutung)
a literary text has / conveys / communicates / transmits **a meaning**
to analyze / interpret / comment on / elucidate / reveal / disclose **the meanning of**
a literary text has a(n) abstract / concrete – **general / particular** meaning
sense
denotes the particular, intelligible (verstehbar) meaning of a word or statement (Sinn, Bedeutung)

a word / statement is used / to be taken / to be understood **in the sense of ...**
it is to be taken in **a literal** (wörtlich) / **figurative** (übertragen) ... **sense**

moral

refers to what a text expressly (ausdrücklich) teaches its readers (Moral)
to state / see **the moral of a story**
the moral of ... (a story ...) is that
a story has / contains / embodies / brings home / **drives home a moral**
to draw / abstract **a moral from ...**
an author **moralizes** on a subject / is a **moralist**

lesson
denotes the (warning or encouraging) experience of an instruction for behaviour that can be had from a text (Lehre, Warnung)
a text contains / teaches / gives a lesson of ... (human behaviour / situations of strain ...)

VI. PROSODY

word field: **prosody / versification** / metrics / rhythmics / verse technique

prosody

denotes the science of versification (Verslehre, Verskunst)
to study / consider / analyze the elements / principles / fundamentals / terms / properties (Eigentümlichkeiten) of prosody
to interpret / elucidate the *prosodic* aspects of a work of art

stanza

denotes a recurring division (wiederkehrender Abschnitt) of a poem which is composed of a uniform (einheitlich) number of lines. The lines (verses) are normally arranged in a fixed pattern of metre and rhyme (Strophe)
a poem is composed of / consists of a number of stanzas
a stanza has / contains / **is composed of verses / lines**
the poet uses / employs / casts his thought in the form of / devises (ersinnen) **a particular kind of stanza** or stanzaic pattern
he employs a(n) couplet (['kʌplit] – Reimpaar; usually a *rhyming*

two-line stanza) / **heroic couplet** (a rhyming couplet of iambic pentameter, often containing a complete thought) / distich (['distik] – a two-line stanza) / **tercet** (a three-line stanza, especially one used as part of a sonnet) / triplet (a three-line stanza, with normally one rhyme) / terza rima (['tɛəsə 'ri:mə] – a dependent three-line stanza, linked by rhyme to the preceding and following stanzas) / **quatrain** (['kwɔtrein] – a four-line stanza) / cinquain (a five-line stanza) / **sestet** [ses'tet] (a six-line stanza) / sestina (a seven-line stanza) / rhyme royal (a seven-line stanza, composed of iambic pentameters) / octave ['ɔktiv] (an eight-line stanza) / ottava rima (an eight-line stanza of iambic pentameters)

a poem is written / composed in couplets / distichs / **tercets** / terza rima / rhyme royal . . .

it is written in the form of the Petrarchan / Shakespearian sonnet (cf. sonnet, p. 64)

a stanza has / is used with **a particular metre / rhythm / rhyme scheme** (rhymes are denoted by small letters: a a b b)

it is used with the iambic / trochaic . . . metre

verse

in its narrower sense, the term *verse* refers to either one metrical line of a poem (Verszeile) or to a whole stanza (Vers, Strophe). As opposed to prose, *verse* also denotes the form of writing collectively defined as poetry (Lyrik, lyrische Dichtung)

a poet makes / writes / composes verses

he says s. th. in verse

a verse contains / consists of / **is composed of a number of accented and unaccented / stressed and unstressed syllables**

it has a number of rhythmical units / feet / measures (Takte)

it has patterned rhythmical units / a metre

a verse flows easily

it runs smoothly (glatt) / **evenly / unevenly**

it runs on into the following verse (line) / **has enjambement**

a sentence comes to an end / ends in the middle of / at the end of a verse

it contains a pause / break / caesura ([si(:)'zjuərə] – a natural pause)

blank verse

is used with reference to a five-stress iambic line without a rhyme

to use / employ blank verse in a play

to write / compose (a play) in blank verse

free verse *(vers libre)*

refers to lines (verses) of uneven length and loose metrical regularity (freier Rhythmus)

to use / employ free verse in a poem
a poem is written / composed in free verse

line

refers to an individual verse within a stanza, a metrical line. *Line* is often used as a substitute for the less clearly defined term *verse* (cf. above)
a poem (stanza) has / contains / **is composed of** / consists of a **number of lines**
the poet uses / employs **lines of the same** / uniform (einheitlich, gleichbleibend) / **different / varying length**

kinds of line
a line has a fixed number of feet / measures (Takt)
it is a monometer (composed of one foot) / dimeter (two feet) / trimeter (three feet) / **tetrameter** (four feet) / **pentameter** (five feet) / **hexameter** (six feet) / heptameter (seven feet) / octameter (eight feet)
the poet uses / employs a(n) **iambic heptameter** / trochaic pentameter (line) . . .
he uses a four-beat / four-stress line with a rising (xx́) / **falling** (x́x) **metre**
there are four / five . . . stresses / beats / accents / lifts **to the line**
a line has an ending (a metrical cadence) / **a weak ending** (ends with an unstressed syllable) / **a strong ending** (ends with a stressed syllable)
a line has / begins with anacrusis ([ˌænəˈkruːsis] – with an unstressed syllable or syllables at the beginning – Auftakt)
it is a four-beat / four-stress line with anacrusis (or an iambic tetrameter)
the sentence overrides (the boundaries of) the verse / line
a poem has (a mixture of) **end-stopped** / (and) **run-on lines** (lines with enjambement)
lines (progressively / regularly / irregularly . . .) **increase / decrease in lenght**

*

rhyme

word field: **rhyme / alliteration / assonance** / consonance / **onomatopoeia**

defining phrases: the term *rhyme,* in its narrow sense, refers to the agreement (Übereinstimmung) / sameness in sound of accented parts of words (Reim) *word family:* **to rhyme** / a rhymester (Verseschmied) – **rhyming** / **rhymeless** / **unrhyming lines**

use (field of collocation):
the verses / **lines of a poem** *rhyme*
they rhyme regularly / **irregularly** / **in pairs** / **alternately** / **successively**
rhymes come / **occur at the end of** / **within lines** – in words in proximity (as in alliteration and assonance)

kinds of rhyme
a stanza has perfect (exact) **rhyme** (has unison [Gleichklang] of vowel and consonant sounds [reiner Reim] – *heard* : *word*)
it has full (rich / echo) **rhyme** (has identical words or homophones with different meaning [rührender Reim] – *sight* : *site*)
it has eye-rhyme (has words identical in writing, but different in sound – *rough* [rʌf] : *bough* [bau])
it has imperfect / approximate **rhyme** (has approximate sameness of consonants or vowels [unreiner Reim] – *snow* : *renew*)
it has slant / **half-rhyme** (rhyme of the consonants – *now* : *know*)
lines have feminine (weiblich) **rhyme** (when the stress falls on the penultimate [vorletzte] syllable – *sénding* : *énding*)
they have masculine (männlich) **rhyme** (when the stress occurs on the final syllable – *tálk* : *wálk*)

rhyme **organizes stanzaic patterns** / **creates tension** / arouses an expectation of a variable end chime (Zusammenklang)
it points forward to / anticipates / **links up** / **suggests a relationship between** / focuses attention on / **contrasts words**
two / three / four lines *rhyme* consecutively
to interpose non-rhyming lines between rhymes
to denote an *unrhymed* line by the letter *x*

a stanza has a RHYME SCHEME
it has **rhyme pairs** (Paarreim) / **cross rhyme** (Kreuzreim – a b a b) / **embracing rhyme** (umarmender / umschließender Reim – a b b a c d d c) / **tail rhyme** (Schweifreim – a a b c c b)

alliteration
is an *initial-rhyme* (Anfangsreim), created by the repetition of initial sounds in two or more words (Alliteration, Konsonantenanreim)
words / the initial sounds of words **alliterate (with each other)**
certain words bear / **carry the alliteration in a line**

assonance [ˈæsəunəns]

is the rhyme of identical or related vowel sounds which are preceded and followed by differing consonants (Assonanz)

to use / introduce **assonance in a line** (such as between *hide* and *time*)

consonance [ˈkɔnsənəns]
is the rhyme of a pattern of identical consonant sounds and differing vowel sounds in words in proximity (benachbarte Wörter) – (*hill* : *hall*) or more loosely of end-consonants alone (*mind* : *hand*)

onomatopoeia [ˌɔnəmætəuˈpiə]
occurs when sounds are somehow imitative of (nachahmen) the thing they refer to (Klangmalerei, Onomatopoesie)
to create / produce **onomatopoeic** / **onomatopoetic effects**
cuckoo [ˈkukuː] is an onomatopoeic word imitating the cry of the bird

*

time

word field: **time** / **tempo** / **beat** (1. the rhythmic strokes within a bar – Taktschlag; 2. the stress, lift on the first syllable of a foot – Hebung) / **metre** / **rhythm**

defining phrases: time, in the prosodic sense, denotes a musical measurement (Messung) of rhythm. It depends upon the number of rhythmic beats (Taktschläge) in successive bars or measures (Takteinheiten) – (Takt, Taktgeschlecht)

word family: to time s. th. (measure / regulate the time of)

use (field of collocation):
to use a duple time (a two-beat group with a stress on the first or second beats; a grouping of two beats – Zweivierteltakt) / **triple time** (a three-beat group – Dreivierteltakt) / **quadruple time** (a four-beat grouping with a primary stress on the first and a secondary stress on the third beat – Viervierteltakt)
to record / **render the time of a bar** / **measure in** (time-measuring) **metrical or musical notation**

to render the time of a bar in **quarter notes** (♩) or an equivalent metrical symbol (such as Heusler's x)
to render the quantity of longer or shorter syllables in a bar in **full notes** (𝅝) / **three-quarter notes** (𝅗𝅥.) / **half notes** (𝅗𝅥) or an equivalent symbol such as Heusler's — / **eighths** (♪) or an equivalent symbol such as Heusler's ∪ / **sixteenths** (𝅘𝅥𝅯) or Heusler's ∩
to divide from each other / indicate **the rhythmical units by bar lines** (vertical strokes)
bar lines separate bars / **measures** / **a group of beats** / **rhythmical units** / **metrical units** / **measures from one strong beat to another**
to count measures from one accented syllable to another

to beat / keep time by the tapping foot
to beat 2/4 / 3/4 / 4/4 (duple / triple / quadruple) time
to count a one-beat rest (𝄽)

rhythm ['riðəm]

| *word field:* **rhythm** / cadence / **intonation** / **metre** / **pace**

defining phrases: in prosody the term denotes a recurrence (Wiederkehr) of stresses at fairly regular time intervals

word family: **rhythm** / rhythmics / **rhythmic**(**al**) / counterpoint rhythm / sprung rhythm

use (field of collocation):
to use / employ / adopt / **create a rhythm**
a poem has / is written in quantitative rhythm (when the duration of syllables is measured, as in Greek metres) / **strong-stress rhythm** (when the force is measured with which words bearing the alliteration are pronounced, as in Anglo-Saxon poetry) / **syllable-stress rhythm** (the standard English metre of accentual verse, i. e. a fixed number of stressed and unstressed syllables)

it is written in sprung rhythm (one stressed syllable is followed by no, or an unfixed number of, unstressed syllables)

to accelerate / **quicken** – decelerate / **slow down** / slacken / **retard** (verzögern) **the rhythmic pace** / **the speed of rhythm** / **the rhythm of a line**
a poem has a flowing / **streaming** / surging (aufwogen) / **dancing** / **skipping** (hüpfend) / **jogging** (schleppend) / **halting** (stockend) / **jerky** (sprunghaft) / **sing-song** / blocking (stauend) **rhythm**
a line has a(n) rising / ascending – **falling** / descending **rhythm**

cadence
denotes either the concluding rhythm of sentences (Kadenz) or, in the normal sense today, the natural rise and fall of the voice in speaking (Sprechrhythmus, Tonfall, Betonung)

to render the cadence / inflexion (melodische Modulation) of the living voice in verse

metre

denotes the fixed pattern of recurring rhythmical units in a verse. In English these are mainly characterized by stress (Metrum)

a poet uses / employs / follows / draws up / fulfils / handles a **metre** / **metrical pattern** / **metrical scheme**

to scan a line / verse in order to bring out / determine **the metrical scheme** / metrical pattern / metrical frame

the basic metrical units are called feet / measures / bars

a line has a duple (2/4) / triple (3/4) / quadruple (4/4) metre the poet employs **a(n) iambic metre** (iamb, -s ['aiæmb]: xx́) / **trochaic metre** (trochee, -s ['trouki:] x́x) / **dactylic metre** (dactyl, -s: x́ ∪ ∪) / **anapaestic metre** (anapaest, -s ['ænəpi:st]: ∪ ∪ x́; the use of the term depends on the technique adopted in dividing metrical units) / **spondaic metre** (spondee, -s: x́x́; a foot used only as a substitute for an iamb or a trochee within a line)

the poet employs a rising metre (a metre which begins with anacrusis, i. e. an iamb / anapaest) / **falling metre** (a metre which falls towards unstressed syllables, i. e. a trochee / dactyl)

a spondee has **a hovering stress** (schwebend) / has level stress – –

*

foot (measure)

| *word field:* **foot** / **bar** / **measure** / **metrical unit** / **rhythmical unit**

defining phrases: in English prosody, the term *foot* denotes a recurrent rhythmical / metrical unit which is composed of stressed / accented and unstressed / unaccented syllables (Fuß). Metrists now often regard the term as ambiguous. They tend to replace it by the terms *bar* or *measure* (Takt)

a poet uses / employs a foot / measure of . . . (two / three syllables)
the poet uses a(n) iambic / trochaic / anapaestic / dactylic / spondaic foot
feet / measures vary in degree of stress
they are composed of weak and strong / stressed and unstressed / accented and unaccented syllables
they contain longs and shorts
feet may be divided by / may contain rests / pauses / a caesura
the place / position of the caesura is / occurs before . . . / after . . .
a caesura is marked by an apostrophe (')

stress

| *word field:* **stress** / **accent** / lift / **beat** / ictus (the stress mark itself)

defining phrases: stress denotes the extra force on a syllable or word used in speaking lines of poetry (Hebung, Ton)

the stress / accent is / falls / occurs / is placed / is required / is expected on the first / second . . . syllable
a word gets / receives a (light / heavy – primary / secondary) stress

stress marks
to indicate stress / accent in a foot by the mark (′ = a single acute) **for a light primary stress** (Haupthebung) **/ a double acute (″) for a** **heavy primary stress** (starke Haupthebung) **/ by the mark (` = a** **single grave) for a light secondary stress** (Nebenhebung) **/ a double** **grave (``) for a heavy secondary stress** (starke Nebenhebung) **on the** **syllable that is stressed – –**

a syllable is lightly / heavily stressed
a word has / gets / receives **/ carries a full – primary / secondary –** **strong / weak** – major / minor – **hovering** (equally distributed stress over two adjacent [benachbart] syllables) **stress**
a word has a wrenched accent (a shift in word accent for the demands of metrical accent)
to juxtapose (nebeneinanderstellen) **stressed words**

syllable

word field: **syllable** / morpheme (a unit of meaning within a word; cf. VII. language)
defining phrases: a *syllable* is a unit of pronunciation in a word which, in prosody, may be described by intensity, duration, and pitch (Silbe)
a syllable requires an amount of time to speak
a sudden increase in the number of unstressed / light / slurred (verschleifen, verschlucken) **/ slack** (schwach) **syllables in a foot quickens** / accelerates **/ increases / speeds up the tempo / rhythm of a line**
syllables are longs or shorts / semi-shorts
a syllable contains a short / long – back / front – dark / high vowel
to stretch (dehnen) **/ drag** (lang ziehen) **/ drawl** (dehnen) / prolong / **lengthen the syllables of a word**
to shorten / compress / **slur** / distort **a syllable in reading / speaking**
to clip (verschlucken) **/ omit syllables in speaking words**
to utter / speak / pronounce a syllable with intensity / force / emphasis
to crowd / jam / crush together (zusammendrängen) **a number of syllables in / into a foot**
a rise / fall in pitch (Tonhöhe) **occurs on a particular** / the preceding (vorausgehend) / the ensuing (folgend) **syllable**

VII. LANGUAGE

word

word field: **word** / vocable / **term** – **expression** / **idiom** / **phrase** / **collocation** / locution

defining phrases: a *word* is one of the basic units of a language (Wort)

word family: **the wording** (of a statement) – (Formulierung, Wortlaut) / **wordy** (a wordy style) – (wortreich) / **word field** / **word family** / **word formation** (Wortbildung) / word sign / word stress / word accent / **word order** (Wortstellung) / word painting (anschauliche Schilderung)

use (field of collocation):

In a situation, from the speaker's point of view

to utter / pronounce / say a word

to mean / express / imply s. th. (andeuten) / **hint at s. th. by a word**

to use / employ a word literally (wörtlich) / **figuratively** (im übertragenen Sinn) – in a certain sense – **in a literal / figurative / generalized sense – in a(n)** extended / transferred / narrow / **wider** sense – **in a derogatory** (abfällig) / pejorative (['piːdʒərətiv] – herabsetzend) **sense**

to look for / hit on (kommen auf) / choose / select a word

to construct / create / **coin** (prägen) **a (new) word**

to give words to s. th. / put s. th. into words / express s. th. in words / apply a word to s. th. / clarify the meaning of a word

to place a word in its proper context / take a word out of its proper context

to quote a word in / out of context

to use a word **in speech / in writing**

to address / speak **words to s. o.**

to bring out / **emphasize** / over-emphasize / **stress** – enrich / **extend** / inforce / place emphasis on / put weight on / **give prominence to the meaning of a word**

to word / reword (neu formulieren) **s. th.**

In a situation, from the listener's point of view

a word is uttered / pronounced / ejaculated (ausstoßen) by s. o.

it rings with a meaning / sense / overtones of

a word conveys a notion / an idea / a concept / an impression / an image of s. th.

the listener / hearer / **reader understands** / **comprehends** / **grasps** / apprehends **the meaning of a word**
he takes a word in the literal / **figurative . . . sense**
a word is effective / equivocal (doppelsinnig, zweideutig) / ambiguous it conveys a double meaning

Words in the context of language generally

WORD FORMATION

a word is composed of letters / **sound units** / phonemes (bedeutungsunterscheidende Laute in gleicher Stellung – **r***ain* : **p***ain*) / morphemes (kleinste bedeutungstragende Einheiten in der Sprache – *call* – **ed**) / **syllables**
it is divided (into syllables) – (trennen)
a word is pronounced with an accent on the (first / **second . . .) syllable**
it is spelt with a hyphen (Bindestrich) / **capital** / **small letter**
a word is hyphenated / constructed (like *gas*) / **given in phonetic transcription** or phonetic notation (like [gæs])
a word has a root / stem / base – is a derivative (Ableitung)
the root of a word has affixes (Affixe) – **prefixed** / **suffixed syllables** – **a prefix** / **suffix** – an ending / termination (final syllable / letter) / a terminal sound (Endlaut)
it has a pronunciation (Aussprache) / **an orthography** / **a spelling**
a word has speech sounds / **vowels** / **consonants** / **semi-vowels** (like [j] / **diphthongs** (like [ai])
a simple / **compound** (zusammengesetzt) – **monosyllabic** / **dissyllabic** / **polysyllabic word**
a contracted form of a word / contraction (like *can't*) – (Kurzform)
a(n) foreign / anglicized / **loan** (Lehnwort) **word**

THE WORD AS A SIGN

a word is a linguistic sign / **symbol**
it is precisely / **loosely applied to . . .**
it is (widely / loosely . . .) applicable
it is a name / symbol for s. th.
it is a key / an approximation to s. th.
a word has a referent (Gegenstück, Bezug) **in the objective world**
it has a(n) meaning / **significance** / **signification** (exact meaning) / sense / bearing on (Beziehung zu) / bearings / import (Sinn) / purport (Bedeutung) / **denotation** (dictionary meaning) / **connotation** (associations / emotional aura)
a word means / **denotes** (bedeuten) / **connotes** (mitbedeuten) / **defines** / **names** / **labels** (etikettieren) / **classifies** / **characterizes** / designates / **specifies** / **entitles** / **describes** / **delineates** / **depicts** / **sketches s. th.**

it signifies / **tells of** / **speaks of** / **points to** / **alludes to** (anspielen auf) / touches on **s. th.**
a word calls forth / **calls up** / **evokes** / **produces** / elaborates **impressions** / **ideas** / **images of**
a word communicates / renders / **conveys** / transmits **a meaning** – **shades of** / **nuances of meaning**
a(n) proper / fitting / suitable / appropriate **word**
the choice of words (Wortwahl)
a key word / catchword (Schlagwort)

THE LINGUISTIC HISTORY OF WORDS

a word has currency in ... (everyday speech)
a word is derived from ... / **of (obscure** / recent ...) **origin** / of (Anglo-Saxon / French ...) derivation / of unknown provenance (['prɔvinəns] – Herkunft)
a word has an etymology / **an acquired meaning**
a word is a(n) archaism / neologism [ni'ɔlədʒizəm] / **barbarism** (schlechter Sprachgebrauch) / **colloquialism** (umgangssprachlicher Gebrauch)
an archaic / obsolete (veraltet) word

SPEECH LEVELS OF WORDS

a word is literary / **formal** / **standard** / **colloquial** / **familiar** / substandard / **dialect** / **slang** (usage)
it is a learned / **technical word**

THE LINGUISTIC CONTEXT OF WORDS

a word is used in / put into / limited by **the context (of other words)**
it is qualified / **modified by another**
a word is a(n) synonym of / **equivalent of** (genaue Entsprechung) / counterpart of – **antonym** / homonym (like *lie* ‚lügen' and *lie* ‚liegen') / homophone (like *tale* and *tail*) – (gleich*lautende* Wörter verschiedener Bedeutung) / homograph (like *lead* [e] ‚Blei' and *lead* [iː] ‚führen') – (gleich*geschriebene* Wörter)

WORDS IN A SENTENCE

a word is (words are) **placed at the beginning** / head / **end** / close **of a sentence**
words are placed in parenthesis – **arranged in a sequence** ['siːkwəns] / **in pairs**
they are grouped in a certain order / into speech-units / **inserted in a sentence** / **juxtaposed** / omitted from a sentence
words precede / **follow each other**
a word heads / **opens** / **closes** / **ends a sentence**
it marks / **signals** the beginning / end / termination of a passage

a word belongs to A WORD-CLASS
it is a(n) noun / verb / adjective
a word is A PART OF SPEECH (Satzglied)
it is the subject / predicate / object
a word enters into collocations (bevorzugte Wortverbindungen) / **phrases / sentences**
the patterns of sentences become fixed in **slogans** (Schlagwort, Werbespruch) / **sayings** (Redensart) / **proverbs** (Sprichwort) / *aphorisms* / *sententiae* (Sentenzen) / *epigrams*

PUNCTUATION IN A SENTENCE

to use punctuation marks to separate sentences / clauses / speech groups ...
to use / omit a(n) full stop (period) / **colon** (:) / **semicolon** (;) / **comma** (,) / **question mark** (?) / **exclamation mark** (!) / **apostrophe** [əˈpɔstrəfi] (') / dash (–) / **round brackets** () / square brackets [] / pointed brackets ⟨⟩ / brace brackets {} / (single) **quotation marks** (inverted commas) ('...') / (double) quotation marks ("...") / ellipsis (three dots / periods) (...) / **a hyphen** (-) / a(n) oblique (slant line) (/) / a wavy line (~)
to write / join words with a hyphen

*

term – (Fachausdruck, Begriff, Bezeichnung)

to use / employ a term
to choose / **define** / fix the meaning of / explain / **apply a term**
to speak of s. th. in plain / exact / intelligible / abusive / evaluating terms
to translate s. th. into rational / critical terms
to use terms interchangeably / **indiscriminately** (unkritisch, unterschiedslos)
a term of detraction (Herabsetzung) / praise
the proper term for ... is ...
terms overlap (s. überschneiden) **in meaning**
a term applies (trifft) / is misapplied
to use a(n) concrete / particular / **abstract** / **commonplace** (Allgemeinplatz) / **generic** (Oberbegriff) / analytical / critical / general / vague / **generalizing** / comprehensive / inclusive **term**
to use a technical / scientific / legal / learned / **literary term**

expression – (Ausdruck)

word family: **to express s. th.** / **expressive** / an express reference to / expressly (ausdrücklich)

to use / employ the most appropriate / a telling (wirkungsvoll) / an odd . . . **expression**
to give expression to s. th.

collocation

stresses the order of words in a phrase. It especially denotes a conventional arrangement of words in a language (Wortverbindung, Kollokation)
words have a (wide / narrow / similar . . .) **range of collocation**
a speaker is familiar with the field of collocation (Bezugs-, Kollokationsfeld) **of a word**
words readily collocate with others / with particular verbs . . .
the word *seat* readily collocates with *to sit on* and *comfortable*
to describe language at the *collocational* level
to test the *collocability* (of a word with others)

idiom

in this context, refers to a phrase or collocation which is peculiar (eigentümlich) to a language. Its individual elements (words) cannot be interpreted literally (wörtlich) – (idiomatische Wendung)
to use / employ an idiom
the idiomatic phrase 'to put up with s. th.' means 'to content oneself with'

phrase

denotes a group of words which frequently recur in the same collocation (Wendung, Redewendung)
to use / employ / have recourse to **a slang / colloquial phrase**
to use a set (fest) / **worn** (abgenutzt) / strained / worn-out / well-worn / **stock** / stale / hackneyed / **trite** (platt) / high-flown (aufgeblasen) **phrase**

figure (of speech)

denotes any of the various expressions used in order to vary / enhance / emphasize / extend meaning (Sprachfigur, rhetorische Figur, Redewendung)
to use / employ concrete figures / **many figures of comparison**
simile / metaphor . . . are figures of speech (cf. VIII. style)

*

vocabulary

denotes a sum or stock (Bestand) of words employed by an individual (author / writer), a group, etc. (Wortschatz, Vokabular)

an author uses / employs / has / possesses / commands a rich vocabulary
he uses a poor / limited / **large / latinized / religious / scientific / technical / descriptive / colloquial / slangy vocabulary**

sentence – (Satz)

word field: **syntax** (ordinary / poetic syntax) / **syntactic(al)** / syntagma (Wörter als Beziehungsträger im Satz, syntaktisch gefügte Wortgruppe)

use (field of collocation):
to form / build / shape / frame / **construct a sentence**
a sentence has a(n) rhythm / flow / cadence / **intonation**
a sentence has a word order / structure / **pattern** / frame / framework
it has the pattern of a(n) statement (Aussage, Behauptung) / **proposition** (Feststellung, Behauptung) / assertion (Behauptung) / **question / command / exclamation / clause / tag question** (angehängte Frage) / answer
it makes a (general / sweeping [zu stark verallgemeinernd] ...) statement / poses a question
it is a declarative sentence (Aussagesatz)
it is a main (Haupt-) / **principal / dependent** (Neben-) **clause**
there are different TYPES OF SENTENCE: **enumerative** (aufzählend, reihend) / **accumulative / coordinate** (bei-, nebenordnend) / paratactic (ds.) / **subordinate** (unterordnend) / hypotactic (ds.) / **elliptical** / one-word **sentences**
there are simple / compound / complex / composite **sentences**
there are periodic / loose sentences

language

word field: **language / tongue (the native / mother tongue)** / vernacular (in the vernacular) – (Landessprache) / **dialect** / idiom (Sondersprache; Ausdrucksweise) / jargon (Fach-, Berufssprache) / register ([situationsgemäßer] Sprachtyp) / **slang** – **speech** (gesprochene Sprache, Rede) / **utterance** (Äußerung) – –
rhetoric (Rhetorik, Redekunst) / **eloquence** (Beredsamkeit, Redegewandtheit) / elocution (Vortragskunst) – –
verbal / linguistic – bilingual (zweisprachig) / polyglot (mehrsprachig)

defining phrases: language, as human speech, is a means of both expressing and communicating thought
It is, as world transferred into the medium of language (gewortete Welt), a system of signs whose referents are to be found in the objective world and the human mind

use (field of collocation):

a language has a vocabulary / grammar / pronunciation / meaning it has a rhythm (a sequence of changes in loudness and length) **/ an intonation** (a continual raising and lowering of the voice)

it has phonological / grammatical / structural / aesthetic features or properties (Merkmale)

it manifests itself in spoken and written forms

to use / employ / speak / handle / master **a language**

the language of a text is precise / exact / plain / simple / denotative (cf. VIII. style)

a speaker uses strong (fluchen) / **bad** / vulgar / **dirty** / obscene / bawdy (zotig) / ribald (obszön, zotig) **language**

he uses stern (streng) / exhortatory (mahnend) / **emotional** / affective / **rational** / austere (herb, schmucklos) / **poetic language**

he uses descriptive / expository (erklärend, darlegend) / **narrative** (erzählend) / argumentative ([ˌɑːgjuˈmentətiv] – logisch, überlegt) **language**

he uses figurative / heightened **language**

he uses forms of the spoken / written language

he does violence to language

some verbs describing the use of language

to utter / speak / call (rufen) / **cry / shout** (laut rufen) **words** – holler (brüllen) / yell / **scream** (schreien) / shriek (kreischen)

to articulate / pronounce / deliver (vortragen, äußern) / ejaculate (ausstoßen) **words**

to repeat / reiterate (ständig wiederholen) **a word**

to swear (at – fluchen) / **curse s. th.** (verfluchen, -wünschen)

to delineate / describe / characterize / portray / picture / **caricature** / distort **s. th.**

to joke / quip (witzeln) / **pun** (e. Wortspiel machen)

to address s. o. – declaim / recite / lecture / sermonize (predigen) s. th.

to talk together with / converse with / confer with s. o.

to enter into / engage in / hold **a conversation with s. o.**

to interrupt s. o. / cut s. o. off in mid-sentence

to ask / pose **a question**

to give a command

to summarize / **sum up** / review / recapitulate / epitomize / condense **s. th.**

to answer / reply (überlegt antworten, erwidern) / **respond** (eingehen auf) / retort (treffend antworten) / echo

to speak to / greet / salute / hail / **invoke** (anrufen, anflehen) **s. o.**

(for non-verbal kinds of utterances cf. voice, p. 20)

verbal adj.
refers to what depends on the medium of words (sprachlich)
verbal art (Wort-, Sprachkunst) / **communication** / **subtleties** / **echoes** / **talent**
to verbalize s. th. (state s. th. in words – in Worte umsetzen, geschickt formulieren)

speech

is usually used with reference to spoken language (Rede, Sprechen)
to use words in speech
to use a prosaic turn of speech
in common / everyday . . . speech

meaning

denotes the relation between linguistic signs and concepts – (Bedeutung)
to define the (literal / explicit / distinct . . .) **meaning of a word**
(cf. V. content and meaning)

VIII. STYLE

word field: **style** / **diction** / **phraseology** / phrasing / **vocabulary** / parlance / **language**

defining phrases: style is created by deviations (Abweichungen) in a writer's manner of expression. It is artistic in its use of (stylistic) figures, but at the same time characteristic of the writer or speaker in its structure – (Stil)
to use / employ / vary a style
to write / speak in a (lucid / clear . . .) style
to mix a style

qualities of style usually considered good
plainness – conciseness – clearness – vigour – elegance

a style is characterized by PLAINNESS (Einfachheit)
it is plain (schlicht) / **simple** / **unaffected** (ungekünstelt)
it is matter-of-fact (sachlich) / sober (nüchtern) / **natural** / severe (herb, schmucklos)

a style is characterized by CONCISENESS (Kürze)
it is concise (knapp, bündig) / **terse** (ds.) / taut (straff) / brief (gedrängt) / **compressed** (ds.) / **condensed** (ds.)

a style is characterized by CLEARNESS (Klarheit)
it is clear / lucid (klar, deutlich)

it is unequivocal (unzweideutig) / **to the point** / **precise** / **definite** / **exact** / descriptive / expository (erklärend) / **concrete** / **vivid** (lebendig, deutlich) / graphic (anschaulich, plastisch)

a style is characterized by VIGOUR (Kraft)
it is vigorous (kraftvoll) / **powerful**
it is impressive / vehement (leidenschaftlich) / **passionate** (ds.)
it is biting / trenchant / incisive (prägnant) / crisp (treffend)
it is lively / spirited (sprühend) / **sparkling** (ds.) / **glowing**
it is weighty (gewichtig) / **ponderous** (ds., schwerfällig)

a style is characterized by ELEGANCE (Eleganz)
it is elegant / **polished** (geschliffen) / classic(al) / restrained (beherrscht, maßvoll)
it is graceful (anmutig) / easy / **fluent** / glib (glatt, gewandt)
it is poetic / **elevated** (gehoben) / sublime (erhaben, hehr) / grand (großartig, gewaltig) / **lofty** (hochfliegend, erhaben)

qualities of style usually considered bad
ornament – diffuseness – obscurity – feebleness – inelegance

a style is characterized by ORNAMENT (Schmuck)
it is ornate ([ɔːˈneit] – geziert, gekünstelt) / pretentious (protzig) / **artificial** (unnatürlich, gesucht) / **mannered** (affektiert, manieriert) / **affected** / **florid** (überladen, blumig) / **flowery** (ds., bilderreich)
it is sonorous ([səˈnɔːrəs] – klangvoll) / **inflated** (geschwollen, schwülstig) / **pompous** (hochtrabend) / **stilted** (ds., gespreizt) / **high-flown** (hochtrabend) / grandiose ([ˈgrændiəus] – ds., bombastisch) ...
it is frothy (leer, schaumschlägerisch) / **flashy** (blendend, unecht) / **slick** (glatt, raffiniert)

a style is characterized by DIFFUSENESS (Langatmigkeit)
it is wordy (wortreich) / verbose ([vəːˈbəus] – ds., weitschweifig)
it is lengthy (langatmig) / **long-winded** (ds.) / **round-about** (umständlich, weitschweifig) / digressive (abschweifend) / **discursive** (ds., unzusammenhängend) / **loose** / **rambling** (weitschweifig, zusammenhanglos)

a style is characterized by OBSCURITY (Dunkelheit)
it is obscure / involved (kompliziert) / **confused** (verworren) / **woolly** (ds., nebelhaft) ...

a style is characterized by FEEBLENESS (Schwäche)
it is weak / **feeble** (kraftlos) / **dry** / **prosy** (nüchtern, trocken) / **bookish** (papieren) / **insipid** (abgeschmackt) / **watery** (wässerig) / **colourless** / vapid (langweilig, geistlos) / **trashy** (kitschig) / trivial / poor / dull ...
it is inexact / **careless** / **lax** (nachlässig) / **slovenly** (schlampig) / **slipshod** (ds.) / slap-dash (ds., oberflächlich)

a style is characterized by INELEGANCE
it is inelegant / **graceless** (plump, schwerfällig) / ungraceful (ds., ohne Anmut)
it is stiff / cramped (ds., verkrampft) / **formal / forced** (gezwungen) / **laboured** (schwerfällig, schleppend) / laborious (ds.) / **ponderous** (ds.) / **awkward** (ds.)
it is banal ([bəˈnɑːl] – abgedroschen) / **trite** (ds., platt, alltäglich) / **cliché ridden** ([ˈkliːʃei] – voller Klischees) / platitudinous (platt, phrasenhaft)

diction

denotes the conscious choice and careful arrangement of words for a particular purpose (for impressiveness, beauty of sound, or phrasing) – (Ausdrucksweise, Diktion)
to use / employ / sustain **the diction of**

some basic stylistic devices (Stilmittel)

figure (of speech)

denotes any of the various expressions used in order to vary meaning (Sprachfigur, Redewendung)
to use / employ a figure

image [ˈimidʒ]

denotes a figure of speech which, in more or less figurative (in übertragener Bedeutung gebraucht) language, conveys a vivid picture to the mind (Bild, bildlicher Ausdruck)
use (field of collocation):
to speak in images
to use / employ / make use of images
to use an image of . . . (corruption / disease . . .) / disease images (imagery)
to use optical / auditory / tactual / kinaesthetic / synaesthetic **images**
to use vivid / ready-made (Klischee-) **images**
to use urban / nautical / dream imagery

pun

denotes a word that suggests two or more meanings simultaneously. It refers to a play upon words that is intended to produce a humorous effect (Wortspiel)
"a mender of bad soles" (Shakespeare, *Julius Caesar,* I. i. 13) is a pun on the homophone [səul] which can mean *sole* or *soul* (the speaker is either a cobbler or a priest)

to use / employ / make a pun on s. th. / a word
to pun on a word / phrase
funny / ingenious / subtle . . . **puns**

*

comparison

in general usage, refers to the linking (Verknüpfung) and likening (Vergleich) of two objects (Vergleich)
to make a comparison between . . . and . . .
a comparison holds / fails
two images / phrases are comparable ['– – –] **in regard to**
to compare s. th. with (a thing of the same class) / to (a thing of a different class)

metaphor ['metəfə]

denotes a(n) implied / reduced (verkürzt) comparison between phenomena of unlike classes (a is b). Metaphor conveys a relation (Beziehung) between two things by using a word (or words) in the figurative (übertragen) sense. It is a poetic means (dichterisches Mittel) of expressing experiences and naming phenomena not so far named by ordinary language (Metapher)
In Shakespeare's *Sonnet 18* the words "the eye of heaven" are a metaphor for *sun* (5: "Sometime too hot the eye of heaven shines")
word family: **metaphoric(al) / to metaphorize s. th.**
use (field of collocation):
to use / employ / resort to metaphor / metaphorical language
spring is often (used as) a metaphor for youth
a metaphor embodies s. th. / calls up a sense of / calls forth associations
to describe / depict s. th. by metaphor
the autumn / summer . . . metaphor
youth is often metaphorized as spring
the *metaphoric* equivalent of youth is spring

symbol

denotes a concrete thing that stands for s. th. immaterial or abstract – (Symbol)
word family: **to symbolize s. th. / symbolic(al) / symbolism**
use (field of collocation):
a symbol presents / represents / stands for s. th.
s. th. is / becomes / serves as a symbol of / for
the rose is a common symbol of love
to use *symbolism*

personification

refers to the attribution (Zuschreibung) of qualities of life to abstract or inanimate (unbelebt) phenomena. It represents them as persons (Personifikation)
personification is implied in the use of the personal pronouns *he* or *she* for things
s. th. is regarded as / represents / is a personification of
to personify s. th.

allegory ['æligəri]

refers to actual figures (Gestalt) or persons used for abstractions (such as virtue / truth / eternity . . .) or for the narrative description of a subject (doctrine / thesis) under the guise (in der Maske) of some other subject (Allegorie)
to use / employ an allegory for
to say / teach s. th. by allegory
to write in *allegoric* fashion
allegorical images / lyric poems
to *allegorize* s. th.

*

repetition

refers to the deliberate using of a word in a text more than once in order to draw attention to them (Wiederholung)
to use / employ / resort to (the figure of) repetition
to say / state s. th. with repetitions
repetition brings out / focuses attention on **implications of words / shades of meaning**
to repeat s. th.

*

exaggeration [igˌzædʒə'reiʃən] – (Übertreibung)

to use exaggeration in saying / stating s. th.
to fall / burst into (baseless / gross . . .) **exaggerations**
a text is full of / abounds in / contains many exaggerations
it is an exaggeration to say / write . . .
to exaggerate s. th.
to make exaggerative statements

an understatement
is a statement in words which *deliberately* express an idea too weakly or inadequately (unzureichend) – (Untertreibung)
"rather nice" is an understatement for "how delightful"
to use an understatement for . . .
to understate s. th. (one's case . . .)

climax

denotes a series of expressions arranged in an ascending scale (steigende Reihe), so that each is more impressive and effective than the preceding. The term may also refer to the last expression in the series – (Höhepunkt, Klimax, Steigerung)
a sentence / paragraph is the / leads up to / rises to / mounts up to / develops to / comes to / reaches a climax
to bring s. th. (a sentence / paragraph / development . . .) **to a climax**
s. th. constitutes a(n) emotional / structural / compositional climax to . . .
to climax a sentence / paragraph by . . .
a paragraph is *climaxed* by . . .

*

euphemism ['juːfimizəm]

refers to the use of a mild (schwach) expression for a(n) unpleasant or cruel one – (beschönigendes Wort, Deckwort, Euphemismus)
"he's passed away" is a euphemism for "he's dead" / "he's a blessed fool" is a euphemism for "he's a damned fool"
to use / employ euphemism(s)

paraphrase ['pærəfreiz]

is the expression of the sense of a text in other words, usually fuller and clearer (verdeutlichende Umschreibung, Paraphrase)
to give / attempt / render **s. th. with / in a paraphrase of**
s. th. is a paraphrase on
to paraphrase ['– – –] **words / a text** (express the meaning of words / a text in other words)
to write in a paraphrastic style

*

allusion

is an indirect or passing reference to s. th. (literature, events . . .) outside the text in which it occurs (Anspielung)
to make an allusion to . . . (the Bible . . .)
s. th. is an allusion to . . .
to use allusive language
to *allude* to s. th.

analogy [ə'nælədʒi]

is the resemblance (Ähnlichkeit) or partial likeness of two or more attributes of phenomena (Ähnlichkeit, Entsprechung, Analogie)
to draw / form / set up / build up / establish / create an analogy between two things

s. th. is / constitutes / develops into an analogy to
s. th. has its analogy in
a paragraph is full of analogies
to draw an *analogical* conclusion
s. th. is analogous to
s. th. is an *analogue* to (forms a corresponding part) / of

antithesis [æn'tiθisis] – (Gegenbehauptung, Antithese)

to use / introduce / develop **an antithesis**
s. th. (**words** / sentences / paragraphs . . .) **form** / constitute **an antithesis to**
paragraphs stand in antithesis

*

irony

is the expression of one's meaning by language of opposite tendency. It refers to the contrast between what is *stated* (for the imcomprehending [nicht verstehen] party of an audience) and what is *suggested* (for the comprehending party of an audience). *Irony* is the contrast between what is said and what is meant (Ironie)
to speak / write / compose / answer / retort **with irony**
to see / understand / comprehend an irony
a text / statement contains (sharp-edged / pungent . . .) **irony**
it is an instance of Socratic irony / **dramatic irony** (tragische Ironie) / **irony of Fate**

parody

is a piece of light writing that imitates the *form and style* of another work in order to amuse or satirize. It is more biting than *travesty* (Parodie)
to give / write / compose a parody of . . . / on . . .
s. th. is a parody of . . . / on . . .
a parody exaggerates / distorts aspects of a serious work

satire ['sætaiə]

is a form of writing that holds up s. th. to ridicule (der Lächerlichkeit aussetzen) – (Satire)
to attack s. th. / s. o. with satire
to write / compose a satire on . . . (in a particular literary form)
to satirize s. th.
to read satirical verse

IX. LITERARY HISTORY

to study the literary works of a(n) age / epoch / era / period / decade / phase – of Greek / Anglo-Saxon / modern . . . times
to study / describe the origin(s) / beginnings / (social / political / literary . . .) **background . . . of an age**
to study the rise / development / flowering / culmination / maturing of an age . . .
to study the changes / decline / disintegration (Auflösung) **/ closing years of an age**
to study a period of transition / the transition from . . . to . . .
to consider the pioneers of / **sources of / influences on /** contributors to / **imitators of the style of a period**
the style of a period has **precursors** (Vorläufer) **/ predecessors** (Ahnherren, Vorfahren)
it is reflected among / copied by / imitated by **the contemporaries** of
it has successors (Nachfolger) / imitators

some literary epochs
to study the literature of antiquity / Anglo-Saxon times / the Middle Ages
to study the literature of the Renaissance [ri'neisəns] / Restoration – of Classicism / Sentimentalism / Rationalism (Enlightenment – Aufklärung) / Romanticism / Realism / Naturalism / the Victorian era / the First World War / the inter-war years / the post-war period
to place / set a work of art in literary history / in a period / in the tradition of . . . (a genre . . .)

groupings of literary works
a work of art is traditional / conventional / eclectic / anachronistic / **revolutionary / modern / avant-garde** ['ævɑ̃ːŋ'gɑːd] **(in outlook / style . . .)**
it is religious / pagan (heidnisch) **/ secular** (['sekjulə] – weltlich) – **popular / courtly** (höfisch) **/ literary / academic**
an author **writes in the vein of** (in der Art) . . .

X. THE AUTHOR

an author, in the literary sense of the word, is a writer of a book / play / novel ...

kinds of author
s. o. is the author / joint author (Mitverfasser) / collaborator (Mitarbeiter) / presumed author **of ... (a book)**
the author can be a lyric poet / sonneteer / lyricist
an author is a minor poet
he is a major / **great poet**
an author is a(n) epic poet / **novelist** / **short story writer** / writer of short stories / **writer of science fiction** / **writer of detective fiction**
he is a dramatist / **playwright** / **play-writer** / **stage-writer**
he is a dramatic author / tragedian / comedian
he is a poet / **writer** / belletrist [–'– –] / script-writer (Drehbuchautor) / **ghost-writer** (one who *ghosts* a book without being named as its real author) / screen writer (for TV)

authorship
an author publishes his works anonymously / **under an assumed name** / **under a pseudonym** ['psjuːdənim]
he uses a *nom de plume* (Schriftstellername) / pen-name / does not write under his real name
an author drafts / projects / **writes a book**
an author's works are published after his death / **posthumously** ['pɔstjuməsli]
to read a posthumous novel ... by / of ...

talent
an author has / **is endowed with** / gifted with **great resourcefulness** (Einfallsreichtum) / ingenuity / **talent** / **genius**
an author is talented / **gifted** / **ingenious** / **resourceful** / **inventive** / **prolific** (produktiv)
he has (vivid / **creative** / **original ...) imagination** / (good / unfailing ...) inspiration
an author becomes the inventor / **founder** (Begründer) / **originator** (Urheber) / **advocate** (Fürsprecher) / promoter (Förderer) **of a mode of writing** / a style / a genre

rank
an author is a distinguished (bemerkenswert) / **good** / **famous** / **great** / **major** / profound **author** / poet
he is a bad / **minor** / **mediocre** (mittelmäßig) **author** / poet

XI. PUBLICATION

word field: **publication** / **edition** / **impression** / compilation (Sammelwerk) / production / **printing**

publication – (Herausgabe, Veröffentlichung)

word family: **to publish s. th.** / **a publisher** / **a publishing house** / **publicity**

use (field of collocation):

to draft a book / play / poem / novel

to bring out / **produce** (herstellen) / **publish** / **edit** / compile (zusammenstellen) / **print a book**

a book presents the original / amended (verbessert) – final / definitive [diˈfinitiv] / **authorized** / **unauthorized** – **an unabridged** (gekürzt) / **abridged** – **complete** / **adapted** (bearbeitet) / emended (emendiert) – **unexpurgated** / **expurgated** (gereinigt) / **bowdlerized** (von anstößigen Stellen gesäubert) / **corrupted** (verderbt) **text**

it is a de luxe ([dəˈluks] – Luxus-) / **scholarly** (wissenschaftlich) / **critical** / variorum / **annotated** (mit Anmerkungen versehen) / library / **popular** (Volks-) / miniature / pirated (Raub-) **edition**

a book contains plagiarisms (words of other authors, used without reference to them)

it is the third / **a corrected** / **revised** (überarbeitet) / **an enlarged** (erweitert) / expanded **impression** / **issue** / **edition**

it is a leaflet (Flugblatt) / **pamphlet** / **booklet** / brochure [ˈbrəuʃjuə] / **paperback** / **soft-cover** / **hard-cover**

parts of a book

a book **has** / **is protected by a** COVER / **front cover** (Vorderdeckel) / **back cover** / **wrapper** / BOOK-(dust-)JACKET / book-band (Reklamestreifen) / case (Kassette)

it is a paperback / **soft-cover** / **hard-cover** / **cloth edition**

a book has a blurb (Klappentext) on the inside flap / jacket flap

the blurb says / claims that . . .

there is a cover title (Umschlagtitel) / title on the spine (auf d. Buchrücken)

a book has PRINTED PAGES

to mark a line / **passage in the margin**

to find a sentence at the top / **in the middle** / **above (below) the middle** / **at the bottom of the page**

the printed page **has chapters** / **paragraphs** / **indentions** (Einrückungen) **at the beginning of (paragraphs . . .)**

it has indented lines
it has chapter headings / subheadings / **asterisk** (Sternchen) (**or footnote) references**
a page has notes / **footnotes** / **annotations** (Anmerkungen) / **a page number**
to read / peruse (sorgfältig durchlesen) / browse (durchschmökern) / **devour** (verschlingen) / pore over (**the pages of**) **a book**
to thumb a book / **skim through** (überfliegen) / glance over **the pages of a book**
to look up a word / quotation **in a book** (dictionary)

kinds of book
to read a FACT BOOK (Sachbuch) / book of fact / book of non-fiction
to use / **consult a** REFERENCE BOOK (Nachschlagewerk) / work of reference / **an encyclopaedia** / a cyclopaedia / **dictionary** / handbook (a guide-book, especially one to an author's works) – (Handbuch) / manual (Handreichung, -buch)
to read a(n) almanac / **magazine** / **journal** / **periodical** (Zeitschrift)
to read a FICTION BOOK / book of fiction / **an anthology** (of poems / short stories ...) / a compilation (Sammelwerk) of ... (interpretations ...)

XII. THE READER / LISTENER

to read a text in silence / **aloud** / **out to s. o.** / **with expression** / with pathos
a work of verbal art is read / **listened to by a**(n) **general** / **unsophisticated** (unverbildet) / unbiased (unvoreingenommen) **reader**
it is read by a man of taste / a literary connoisseur [ˌkɔniˈsəː]
it is read by a systematic critic / an analyst / a scholar / **a reviewer** (Rezensent)
it is read by a(n) amateur / dilettante [ˌdiliˈtænti]
to realize the meaning of a text on first / **second reading**
the reader responds to / is alive to / is sensitive to / is aware of the implications of a text
he responds with sensitiveness / judgment – with attention to / perception of / a grasp of / comprehension of / apprehension of detail and technique
a text communicates a meaning to the reader
it develops his sensibility / influences his attitude towards his fellowmen and his environment
it impresses his mind with verbal moulds of perception

INDEX OF KEY TERMS

English

C

D

INDEX OF KEY TERMS

German – English

Z